To my sister, Nancy Louise Bruner, with love.
Her moral support and constant encouragement
enabled me to complete this project.

ABOUT THE AUTHOR

Ruth Ellen Kinzey, MA, is a full-time Lecturer at the University of North Carolina in the Communications Studies Department, where she teaches courses in public relations, public speaking, and journalism. She also teaches seminars on writing effective newsletters, speakers bureaus, and community relations for Duke University's Nonprofit Management Certification Program. In addition, she is a public relations/marketing consultant for nonprofit agencies and for-profit businesses, as well as an executive speech coach and a professional public speaker. Ms. Kinzey has won numerous awards for her newsletters, annual reports, direct mail pieces, and crisis communication plans. Her many speaking engagements have included the Annual Conference of the National Society of Fund Raising Executives for Virginia and North and South Carolina where she lectured on "How to Focus a Marketing Effort," the North Carolina meeting of the International Association of Administrative Professionals where she asked members "Are You Ready for the New Millennium?" and, in June of 2000, the annual conference of the International Communication Association in Acapulco, Mexico, where she will speak on a panel entitled "Planned Change, Unplanned Challenges: Insights from the Organizational Front Lines." Ms. Kinzey is a member of Public Relations Society of America, International Association of Business Communications, and Women in Communication. She is a graduate of Coe College with a BA in speech, English, and secondary education, and a graduate of the University of Iowa with an MA in journalism with a concentration in public relations.

Using Public Relations Strategies to Promote Your Nonprofit Organization

HAWORTH Marketing Resources
Innovations in Practice & Professional Services
William J. Winston, Senior Editor

New, Recent, and Forthcoming Titles:

Using Public Relations Strategies to Promote Your Nonprofit Organization

Ruth Ellen Kinzey, MA

Routledge
Taylor & Francis Group
NEW YORK AND LONDON

First Published by

The Haworth Press, Inc., 10 Alice Street, Binghamton, NY 13904-1580

Transferred to Digital Printing 2008 by Routledge
270 Madison Ave, New York NY 10016
2 Park Square, Milton Park, Abingdon, Oxon, OX14 4RN

Softcover edition published 2000.

Material taken from *Six Keys to Recruiting, Orienting, and Involving Nonprofit Board Members*, by Judith G. Nelson, © 1997 by the National Center for Nonprofit Boards, is reprinted with permission. For more information about NCNB, write to 1828 L. Street NW, Suite 900, Washington, DC 20036-5104, telephone (202) 452-6262, 1-800-883-6262, fax (202) 452-6299, e-mail ncnb @ncnb.org, or visit the website at www.ncnb.org.

Cover design by Marylouise E. Doyle.

The Library of Congress has cataloged the hardcover edition of this book as:

Kinzey, Ruth Ellen.
    Using public relations strategies to promote your nonprofit organization / Ruth Ellen Kinzey.
      p. cm.
    Includes bibliographical references and index.
    ISBN 0-7890-0257-4 (alk. paper)
    1. Nonprofit organizations—Management. 2. Public relations. I. Title.
HD62.6.K536 1999
659.2'88—dc21
                                                           99-17249
                                                           CIP

ISBN 0-7890-0258-2 (pbk.)

Publisher's Note

CONTENTS

Preface

While pursuing my master's degree in journalism at the University of Iowa, I selected the topic of nonprofit annual reporting for my thesis. My decision to do this was twofold. First, I had learned a great deal about annual reporting through my experience in the corporate world, and I wanted to "formalize" my training. More important, I assisted nonprofits through my volunteer work. In doing so, I was surprised to see how few of these organizations felt the need to prove fiscal responsibility to their "investors."

After thinking about it, I realized these small nonprofits did not produce an annual report because they were so busy focusing on fundraising and day-to-day issues that they didn't have time to think about such a document, much less produce one. Also, the annual report was "new territory" for a staff member who already wore many different hats. This person might be handling marketing, fund-raising, public relations, training, and assisting the executive director. Therefore, this person was probably hired for experience and skills other than those required to produce a sophisticated document such as an annual report.

While conducting my master's research, I also became increasingly aware that competition among nonprofits was becoming keener. Clearly this trend would continue. That was in 1989 and 1990.

Since then, allegations of misuse of funds by some nonprofit leaders have forced all nonprofits to rebuild the public trust eroded by these few. Donors and volunteers now ask more questions, check the validity of a nonprofit's request, and scrutinize the financial and organizational reputation of the independent sector.

While the level of donor and volunteer sophistication increases, many small nonprofits still find themselves hiring a single individual to perform multiple tasks. These persons may or may not possess training or experience in the public relations field yet find themselves accountable for such programs and projects. In this scenario, assigned persons may give perfunctory performances but are unable to execute these assignments strategically.

Recognizing the dichotomy of the situation—an increasingly competitive environment that requires the critical public relations skills found in business juxtaposed against the employee assigned multiple responsibilities with minimal, if any, public relations or marketing training—this book is designed to help small nonprofits recognize the value of strategic public relations and to help the novice employee ascertain "the basics" of a few specific efforts.

One area of discussion in this book is the annual report. What I discovered in 1989 and 1990 is even more relevant today, and those nonprofits that do not produce an annual report should do so.

A second subject is newsletters. Although most nonprofits have at least one newsletter, this print medium is not used as strategically as it should be. Therefore, one chapter discusses the strategic aspects of newsletters and how to make this communication vehicle more effective.

The speakers bureau is a public relations program that most nonprofits have. Unfortunately, it may be purely by accident: the organization received a telephone call and sent someone to "talk about" the nonprofit. Such an approach is not effective, much less strategic. Therefore, a chapter describes how to set up a speakers bureau, strategically market it, and monitor its effectiveness.

Finally, in a small nonprofit, the person assigned the nonprofit's public relations duties typically provides support to or becomes involved with the nominating, training, and educating of board of director members. Those involved with nonprofit board development and succession planning must take their cues from for-profit business. Simply to have a "warm body" fill a seat is not sufficient logic either to recruit someone to join a board of directors or to leave the person on the board. Personnel must be strategically selected and recruited for these seats and developed and trained to optimize their volunteer contributions. In addition, the nonprofit needs a succession plan for leadership development. Chapter 5 addresses these issues and describes the role public relations can play in the process.

The field of public relations contributes in many other ways to the nonprofit arena. Other PR vehicles used by nonprofits include media relations, crisis communications, government relations, community relations, and special events. However, it is my hope that by addressing a few PR components, this book will assist the novice nonprofit communicator to perform these basic public relations tasks effectively and strategically. It is also my hope that a nonprofit's executive director and president will understand the valuable role of public relations and how this discipline complements marketing and fundraising to produce even greater results.

Acknowledgments

A special thanks to the following persons for their assistance with this endeavor: Joseph E. Gettys, my husband; David C. Burkhardt, CADMUS Financial Communications, Raleigh, NC; John Daughtry, KPC Photography, Charlotte, NC; Sandy Dempsey, Corporate Reports, Atlanta, GA; Nancy Jean Frees, The Frees Foundation, Houston, TX; Elaine Lyerly, The Lyerly Agency, Charlotte, NC; Marilyn MacKenzie, The Duke Endowment Library, Charlotte, NC; Dawn Michelle Miller, Charlotte, NC; Dustin Peck, KPC Photography, Charlotte, NC; Margie Storch, Storch Design, Charlotte, NC; Barbara Voorhees, The United Way of Gaston County, Gastonia, NC; W. Jamie Ward, Visual-Eyes, Cedar Rapids, IA; Wes Westmoreland, Westmoreland Printers, Inc., Shelby, NC; and Larry Zeigler, Photographer, Gastonia, NC.

Chapter 1

The Nonprofit Entity and Business PR

DEFINING NONPROFIT

Defining "nonprofit" is a difficult task, because it is not part of the public nor the private domain. It is a separate entity that operates somewhere between the two. If analyzing the not-for-profit sector on an informal basis, many similarities are found between it and for-profit corporations. A well-run nonprofit engages in planning, budgeting, accounting, and marketing. It must deal with personnel, information management, and governance issues. However, long-range planning, financial reporting, and organizational accountability, unlike in private business, are not based on the economic advancement of those who provide its capital. Although nonprofits must be financially soluble and even entrepreneurial in spirit, their primary objective is not to make money for their owners or shareholders. Profits are used to meet the organization's public service objectives. [1]

There are a few truisms about nonprofits. First, it is important to remember that a nonprofit organization is a nongovernmental entity, legally constituted and incorporated under state law as a charity or not-for-profit corporation. The governance structure of the nonprofit precludes self-interest and private gain but must serve some public purpose.

Federal income tax is not paid because the nonprofit possesses tax-exempt status. According to the IRS, [2] to be tax-exempt under federal law, an organization must satisfy organizational and operational tests. The organizational test examines the group's two governing documents: one that creates the nonprofit and one that specifies the rules of operation. This information categorizes the tax-exempt entity into one of three types: the not-for-profit corporation, the trust, and the unincorporated association.

The operational test checks to ensure that the organization's operations conform to the requirements of the particular tax-exempt classification. This check assesses if too much lobbying is occurring, if political campaign activities are taking place, or if net earnings are going to individuals in a private capacity. In short, the operational test relates to the ongoing operations of the nonprofit. The agency also possesses a special legal status stipulating that donations made to the charity are tax deductible. [3]

It should be noted that the Internal Revenue Service has twenty-five separate categories of tax-exempt organizations. Included in this universe are the 501 (c)(3) and 501(c)(4). The IRS code defines the 501(c)(3) classification as religious, educational, charitable, scientific, and literary organizations, and those testing for public safety, fostering certain national or international sports competitions, or working to prevent cruelty to children or animals. It also includes private foundations as part of the independent sector universe.

The 501(c)(4) category includes civic leagues, social welfare organizations, and local associations of employees. These nonprofits promote community welfare or charitable, educational, or recreational activities and are part of the independent sector. [4] Although this book targets 501 (c)(3) and 501(c)(4) entities, it stresses the importance for all nonprofits to adopt a business-like public relations approach.

THE GROWTH FACTOR

The declining confidence in government's ability to address social ills places an even greater demand on nonprofits. The result? An ever-growing number of social service agencies, hospitals, educational institutions, environmental groups, health organizations, and religious entities are founded within not-for-profit parameters. [5] The growth is clearly evident in annual reference materials such as *Giving and Volunteering in the United States*, *Giving USA*, and the *Nonprofit Almanac.* These publications provide statistical updates and trend information on the nonprofit sector.

Giving and Volunteering in the United States (1996) also summarizes the significant change in public attitude regarding government's role in caring for those who cannot care for themselves. In

1988, eight of ten survey respondents agreed this was a government responsibility. Yet in 1996, only six out of ten agreed. These numbers demonstrate a 25 percent decline in the percentage of respondents agreeing with this statement. A declining majority of Americans also hold the same attitude about money the government spent to help the poor. [6] If the public believes it is not the role of government to help those unable to help themselves, this task inevitably falls on the private domain.

Likewise, the percentage of the individuals *disagreeing* with the statement, "Most charitable organizations are wasteful in their use of funds," is up from 1990 to 1996. However, the 1996 percentage reflects a slight decline over 1994 figures. This demonstrates that, overall, public perception is returning to favor nonprofit performance, but reservations remain. [7]

To better understand this fluctuation in trust, it is necessary to assume a historical perspective. In the early 1990s, a few noteworthy instances caused the public to question the reputation of nonprofits. For example, in 1990 the media reported an accusation that Father Bruce Ritter, the Franciscan priest who founded Covenant House in New York, misused the agency's funds and also called his personal conduct into question. Although an investigation determined that funds were not misused, the organization had to work hard to regain the public's trust. [8] In 1992, the United Way of America scandal rocked the nonprofit world, causing many to scrutinize all nonprofits. The agency's president, William Aramony, resigned after allegations of inappropriately spending United Way funds. Aramony was convicted of embezzlement. [9] Even the Girl Scouts of America weathers a periodic accusation that too large a share of cookie sale profits are earmarked for administrative support.

Instances such as these grab media attention and produce a cascading effect on both large and small organizations. To continue the growth curve, nonprofits must be conscious of their individual reputation as well as the image of this sector on a nationwide basis. By taking proactive measures to establish an impeccable reputation and circumvent the possibility of a negative association, a control factor is introduced to help ensure the success of the individual organization and the sector as a whole.

HUMBLE BEGINNINGS TO BIG BUSINESS

Prior to 1900, twelve national organizations solicited funds. They were:

- Young Men's Christian Association
- National Women's Christian Temperance Union
- International Sunshine Society
- The Salvation Army
- American Red Cross
- Needlework Guild
- Young Women's Christian Association
- American Humane Association
- Council of Jewish Women
- National Children's Home Society
- National Florence Crittendon Mission
- National Consumers' League

Between 1900 and 1916, twenty more national agencies were born, including the National Tuberculosis Association, Boy Scouts of America, Camp Fire Girls, Girl Scouts, and National Committee for the Prevention of Blindness. [10] Since then, the number of local and national nonprofits has skyrocketed. In 1996, 1,530,000 nonprofits existed, up from 1,123,000 in 1977. Further examination of these numbers indicates extensive growth in the 501 (c)(3) category.

Placement of trust in the nonprofit sector to accomplish what the public thinks government cannot or should not encourages a trend of continued growth in the number of organizations, financial contributions, and volunteerism.

Independent Sector Organizations [11]		
	1996	**1992**
Total number, including religious institutions, 501(c)(3), 501(c)(4), and other tax-exempt organizations	1,135,000	1,030,000
501(c)(3)	654,000	546,000
501(c)(4)	140,000	143,000

Today, nonprofit organizations *are* big business. In 1997, more than 692,500 charities were registered with the Internal Revenue Service as a 501 (c)(3) corporation. [12] That same year, approximately 93 million United States adults supported these entities through 20.3 billion hours of volunteer time, with a value of $201 billion. [13] In 1997, Americans financially supported these same nonprofits with an estimated $143.6 billion, [14] a figure that represents 1.8 percent of the gross domestic product. [15]

When reviewing these statistics, it is also worthy to note that all financial gifts originate from four sources that have varied little over time. Foundations and corporations have supported nonprofits, with foundations providing slightly more support than companies. However, individuals, through a lifetime of support and willed contributions, have provided approximately 85 percent of the charitable support over the past three decades. Consequently, routine individual donations and bequests play a critical role in the finances of nonprofits. [16]

Demands placed on nonprofits are linked directly to the changing social and economic realities with which we are faced, not only in the United States, but on a worldwide basis. For that reason, the nonprofit sector even competes internationally with business in regard to size. Johns Hopkins Comparative Nonprofit Sector launched a project in 1990 that collected and analyzed data from twelve countries: the United States, the United Kingdom, France, Germany, Italy, Hungary, Japan, Brazil, Ghana, Egypt, Thailand, and India. The findings revealed the nonprofit sector to be a major economic force, employing 11.8 million workers in seven countries. This accounted for one of every twenty jobs and one out of every eight service positions. Nonprofit employment in these countries exceeded the combined employment of the largest private company in each individual country by a factor of six to one. The United States also claims the largest segment of the nonprofit employment category, listing 6.9 percent of the total opportunities. [17]

Recognizing the scope of the nonprofit sector, it is easy to understand why Philip Kotler and Alan Andreasen, in *Strategic Marketing for Nonprofit Organizations* , describe the plight of the small nonprofit: "Small charities and other nonprofit organizations have great difficulty getting the world to pay attention to them. They compete with hundreds of other organizations clamoring for newspaper space and air time for their equally important stories and events. Small organizations all too often get lost in the deluge of public relations material that reach media gatekeepers every day." [18]

EVALUATIONS ARE IN PLACE

With the proliferation of charities, some of which are not legitimate and some of which have fiscal and management problems, contributors and volunteers are tempted to assume a "donor beware" attitude. In fact, a level of frustration in this area was voiced by law enforcement and charity officials. [19] Because of their frustration in dealing with shady and fly-by-night fund raisers and charities, the National Association of Attorneys General spearheaded legislation for a state act concerning the solicitation of funds for charitable purposes in 1986. On June 29, 1988, the efforts became unimportant because of a U.S. Supreme Court opinion by Justice Brennan in *Riley v. National Federation of the Blind of North Carolina, Inc.* This case clarified and expanded the First Amendment protection for solicitation by nonprofit organizations and their right to utilize professional fund-raisers. With the ruling, the Court removed any lingering doubts about whether government could limit the fund-raising expense of charities, prohibit point-of-solicitation disclosure of fund-raising costs, and require that the licensing of any professional fund-raisers must be expedient   (with provision for prompt judicial review).[20]

Given what happened in the 1980s, yet recognizing the level of frustration regarding the misrepresentation and misuse of the nonprofit status and fund-raising techniques, the National Charities Information Bureau (NCIB) created nonprofit evaluation standards. The standards offer a way for the public to determine if a charity is a worthwhile cause and should receive support. A rating scale, based on nine standards, addresses two broad categories: (1) governance, policy, and program fundamentals, and   (2) reporting and fiscal fundamentals. Requirements include:

- An unpaid board of independent volunteer directors, with no fewer than five voting members who meet at least twice a year.

Other stipulations state that members should have no conflict of interest; no more than one paid staff person can be on the board; a majority of members must attend each meeting; and an individual attendance policy is in effect.

- A formal statement of purpose approved by the board of directors.
- Activities must be consistent with the statement of purpose.
- All promotion, fund-raising, and public information must accurately describe the organization's identity, purpose, programs, and financial needs.
- Fund-raising practices cannot be intimidating. Financial information for all income and revenue-generating activities must be available upon request.
- At least 60 percent of expenses must be applied to the charity's programs. Net assets cannot exceed twice the current year's expenses or the next year's budget.
- An annual report must be available upon request. It should contain explicit narratives of the organization's major activities during the period covered by the audited financial statements.
- A detailed annual budget, consistent with the classifications in the audited financial statement and approved by the board, should be on file. [21]

The NCIB publishes a guide offering detailed reports on individual charities. *Wise Giving Guide* offers an independent assessment as to how a national charity spends its donated funds. [22]

Not only has the lack of trust in nonprofits manifested itself through the custom of rating a nonprofit's worthiness, a noteworthy trend has materialized in the individual donor category as well. Donors want to be able to select specific charities in workplace-giving campaigns. [23] Therefore, organizations that represent more than one nonprofit have had to provide donors with individual agency options.

ADOPTING A BUSINESS STRATEGY

All of these data testify to exactly how large the nonprofit business is, the high level of competition that exists in this sector, and the need for individual organizations to prove themselves as credible and worthy to be supported by donors. Yet despite the numbers and the obvious competition for volunteer time and contributions, not all nonprofits have adopted a businesslike approach. Words that are part of corporate nomenclature—such as total quality management, re-engineering, aggressive marketing, succession planning, and collaboration—are just beginning to be uttered by nonprofits.

No longer can nonprofits rely on past achievements or the goodwill of the public. With greater frequency, nonprofits must prove "worthy of investment," as "stockholders" want to see their "dividends" materialize in the form of a better community or an improved living environment. For this reason, not-for-profit corporations should:

- Clearly define their purposes and goals.
- Create comprehensive financial plans.
- Respond to change by adjusting services and programs that are meaningful to their constituency and to the community at-large.
- Evaluate operations to assess effectiveness.
- Achieve consensus on controversial issues.
- Collaborate with business, government, and other nonprofits whenever possible.
- Obtain as well as retain quality volunteers and staff.
- Communicate goals, needs, and successes internally and externally.

This strategic and businesslike approach eliminates the possibility of a nonprofit being governed simply by the whimsy of a single board member and keeps the "market niche," regarding the public service objectives and the competing nonprofits, in perspective. This approach fosters agenda-setting, benchmarking, and ongoing measurement to ensure the organization is progressing and meeting the needs of its clients in the most effective manner possible. In fact, once a strategy is developed, the nonprofit should utilize this information in its marketing and public relations plans. This increases the likelihood that the agency will meet its goals and advance along a continuum of success while building public trust.

MARKETING THE NONPROFIT

Because of increased competition for financial and volunteer support, the reputation of nonprofit entities, and the public's expectations of the independent sector, the role of nonprofit marketing increases in significance. Therefore, it is advisable for nonprofits to adhere to the same marketing principles that for-profit businesses use. The first step in this process is to understand what the nonprofit does and how this compares to the performance of competing organizations. To achieve this, a market description must be developed, and the competition must be analyzed. These efforts require research. In some cases, extensive research may be necessary to produce sufficient data for thorough market analysis and trends to become apparent. This step is well worth the time and monetary investment, as it ultimately illustrates the "big picture" in which the individual nonprofit operates. Once they grasp the function of the individual agency in this broader context, marketing, public relations, and fund-raising personnel can develop a strategically devised promotional plan, rather than rely solely on guesswork.

Armed with research and knowing the goals and objectives of the nonprofit, personnel can begin the planning process for the aforementioned functions, making sure marketing, public relations, and fund-raising are integrated into a team approach. A strategically planned program can be developed by adhering to the basic components found in a planning, communication, and evaluation matrix (see Figure 1.1). By addressing each of the steps in this model, several important factors come to light that impact the success of these three organizational functions. For example, are there negative associations with the nonprofit? Does the public have any uninformed or negative perceptions about the organization? Which publics actively seek to work with the nonprofit? Are there barriers that impede the agency's successful implementation of a campaign or project? Can collaboration opportunities be identified? And finally, where should this campaign, project, or program be assigned—marketing, public relations, or fund-raising?

FIGURE 1.1. Steps in a Strategic Planning Program Matrix

- Background, synthesizing primary and secondary research on the non-profit industry, market situation, current trends, opinions and attitudes, etc.
- Situation analysis, clearly stated in a single paragraph
- Central core of objective or difficulty
- Preliminary identification of publics
- Preliminary identification of resources
- Specific program or campaign goals
- Objectives
- Specific identification of key publics
- Message design
- Strategies to reach each public
- Tactics or tools to support each strategy
- Calendar in the form of a time-task matrix, including program implementation
- Budget, specifying the cost of each tactic
- Communication confirmation to ensure the stipulated message reaches each public
- Identification of evaluation criteria to measure the success of the campaign or program
- Evaluation tools to measure each, including a calendar and budget

Source: Laurie J. Wilson, *Strategic Program Planning.* Dubuque, IA: Kendall-Hunt Publishing Co., 1997, p. 15.

WHAT IS PUBLIC RELATIONS?

Numerous books on nonprofit fund-raising are already on the shelves. Articles and texts addressing nonprofit marketing appear with increasing frequency. However, the concept of applying the same strategic public relations methodology used in business to the nonprofit world has experienced limited discussion, thus far.

Public relations professionals work in a variety of fields such as investor relations, issues management, media relations, community relations, membership relations, special events management, protection of organization's reputation and image enhancement, publicity, public affairs, employee communication, and crisis communication. Consequently, numerous public relations strategies and tactics can be used by a nonprofit to enhance its reputation, complement its marketing plan, and contribute to its fund-raising success. However, the scope of this book is limited to four particular assignments and the role the public relations professional plays in each. But before examining specifics, a discussion of public relations as a discipline and how it compares to the marketing function is in order.

According to Cutlip, Center, and Broom in the sixth edition of their book *Effective Public Relations,* "Public relations is a management function that identifies, establishes, and maintains mutually beneficial relationships between an organization and the various publics on whom its success or failure depends." [24]

Public relations is a planned and deliberate process that includes research and analysis, policy and procedural formation or recommendation supporting public interest, and communication with and feedback from numerous publics. Communications professor John Marston describes the PR effort through an acronym, RACE, in which he identifies four specific functions assigned to public relations: Research, Action, Communication (and planning), and Evaluation. [25]

This process is most successful when it adheres to a two-way symmetrical model developed by Todd Hunt and James E. Grunig. These two researchers suggest that public relations is most successful when a two-way, balanced communication is aimed at producing mutual understanding. Research and communication are used to manage conflict, permitting negotiation and compromise to improve the understanding with strategic publics as well as to ensure an ethical approach. [26]

Public relations is not the same as marketing, advertising, or journalism. Each category has its own domain. Kotler and Andreasen observed: "The recent emergence of marketing as a 'hot topic' in nonprofit circles has raised a major question in the minds of chief administrators and public relations managers as to the relationship between marketing and public relations in a nonprofit organization. Clearly, the two functions work well together in business firms with marketing focusing on the development of plans to market the company's products to consumers, while public relations takes care of relations with the publics. In nonprofit organizations, the relationship between the public relations and marketing departments has been marked by tension due to a lack of clearly defined areas of responsibility." [27]

Because confusion often arises in nonprofits concerning the responsibilities of public relations practitioners and marketing personnel, job descriptions must be differentiated. At the same time, it is apparent how the two disciplines must work as a team to ensure success.

Perhaps the differences are most clearly seen when comparing public relations with other disciplines. For example, marketing is a process that attracts and satisfies customers or clients on a long-term basis so as to achieve the firm's economic objectives. [28] Advertising creates and places paid media messages. [29] The objective of journalism is to gather and select information with the primary purpose of providing objective information and news to a mass audience. [30]

A specific illustration of how public relations and marketing approach a single project from two different angles is the area of promotion. A marketer uses an event and related activities to call attention to how a user's needs are met by specific goods or services. A public relations practitioner utilizes promotion to build beneficial associations with various publics through selected events and activities. Another example is a special event. A marketer stages events to publicize the benefits of a service or product offered by the company. Public relations, in its purest form, stages the special event to win publicity for its goal of relationship development. [31]

Ultimately, nonprofit PR professionals communicate with various publics in an effort to influence the knowledge, attitudes, and behavior of and toward the organization. [32] These practitioners have goals such as developing public support for an issue, changing the perception of the organization, influencing legislation, building a coalition, or supporting a fund-raising campaign. [33] As David Rados explains, these goals translate into a myriad of activities:

- Training and development of volunteers and staff.
- Combating rumors.
- Appearing before government commissions.

- Handling special events such as anniversaries, awards ceremonies, appreciation dinners, open houses, etc.
- Making films and videos.
- Working with editors and answering reporter questions.
- Lobbying.
- Writing letters.
- Ghosting correspondence.
- Training and development of board and staff.
- Handling complaints.
- Running a speakers bureau.
- Writing newsletters and brochures.
- Preparing annual reports. [34]

A seven-step strategic planning model, outlined by Philip Kotler and Alan Andreasen, is recommended to ensure public relations success in these endeavors (see Figure 1.2).[35] Use of this basic plan increases awareness of the organization, already noted to be a major challenge for nonprofits, and produces very specific results identified as being desirable and measurable goals.

FIGURE 1.2. Seven-Step Strategic Planning Process

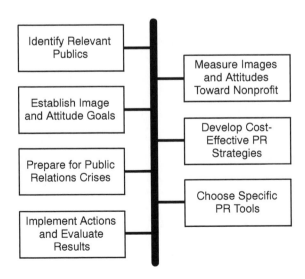

Subsequent chapters address four public relations endeavors: annual reports, newsletters, speakers bureaus, and strategic board member selection and training. Some components within the seven-step public relations model will be discussed and specific "how-to" comments on the development of each public relations measure will be outlined.

Chapter 2

The Annual Report

The annual report is an important communications tool with public relations value. Because of federal government standards, publicly traded companies in the United States are required to disclose financial information. These institutions rely on the annual report to disseminate their financial performance as well as to tell the stories behind the numbers. In fact, according to a survey conducted by Potlatch Corporation, these organizations consider the annual report to be the single most important document produced by their companies, ranking it ahead of all other media tools, including sales brochures and advertising. [1] Even many private businesses issue an annual report for public relations and marketing reasons.

If firms not required to print such a document recognize its importance, why shouldn't nonprofits use this communications tool to solicit potential donors, some of which are businesses? The answer: Nonprofit organizations should publish an annual report as part of their public relations and marketing plans. In fact, back in 1991, a representative of the American Cancer Society stated: "The annual report is critical, and we use it to support just about everything we do. It is the primary vehicle for reaching new volunteers unfamiliar with what we do, it thanks donors for their help throughout the year, and it shows where and how our funds have been spent." [2]

A PUBLICLY TRADED PERSPECTIVE

Firms traded on the stock exchanges comply with stringent financial reporting procedures. Published annually by public corporations, the annual report reflects the financial status of an organization. Financial reports include a balance sheet, income statement, stockholder's equity, cash flow statements, and auditor's report. Usually, the chairman of the board and president comment on events impacting the firm's financial results during the past year. The report is primarily written for the company's shareowners, but it is issued to all interested parties. So, a diverse group receives this publication.

The concept of disclosure for nonprofits is a broad one. Alan Afterman and Rowan Jones discuss the level of disclosure required and/or suggested for such organizations in their 1993 publication *Nonprofit Accounting and Audit Disclosure Manual* . According to Afterman and Jones, only a few Financial Accounting Standards Board (FASB) Statements refer explicitly to nonprofits. However, the generally accepted accounting principles (GAAP) have comprehensive guidelines established for these organizations based on the same standards used for commercial, service, and industrial companies. Manuals, such as those developed by Afterman and Jones, guide the not-for-profit entity in recording, retaining, and filing pertinent financial information. [3]

Producing an annual report, then, becomes a fairly easy task for nonprofits to accomplish, since these organizations already compile financial data. A narrative describing the agency and its goals is added to this material, which results in a communications medium in which the nonprofit justifies its existence on an annual basis. It also provides an opportunity for the agency to showcase itself, explaining how the organization contributes to the well-being of the community.

A review of established annual reporting practices in the corporate world coupled with a perusal of reports from other nonprofits reveals much about what financial information and which facts to disclose. What components are typically found within a corporate annual report?

- Financial highlights containing a two-year or three-of-five year comparison.
- A narrative review of annual operations, frequently by segment or product line.
- A narrative section showcasing the company's strengths or strategies.
- A management report with discussion and analysis.
- A five-year summary of selected financial data.
- An annual statement of consolidated income.

- An annual consolidated balance sheet.
- An annual statement of stockholder's equity.
- An annual statement of cash flow.
- A financial review of fund sources and applications.
- A schedule of long-term debt.
- A schedule of capital stock.
- Notes to consolidated financial statements.
- An opinion of a certified public accountant.
- A list of corporate subsidiaries.
- A list of senior officers.
- A list of directors with individual affiliations and titles noted. (Board committees on which the director serves and number of board meetings attended can also be included.)
- A corporate profile.
- A letter from the chairman and CEO.
- Notice of the annual meeting.
- Corporate address, phone number, fax, transfer agent, accounting firm, investor contact, dividend policy, quarterly stock price information, and stock exchange listing.
- Equal opportunity employer statement.
- Table of contents.
- A statement of company trademarks.
- Credit design firm, illustrator, and photographer (optional but frequently done, if name talent is utilized).

This comprehensive list seems intimidating to the novice public relations practitioner. However, it is essential to remember two facts:

1. Nonprofits are not required by law to disclose the same detailed financial operating results and company data nor in the same format that publicly held corporations must.
2. Not all of these components are applicable to an agency and/or are appropriate for a nonprofit audience.

Consequently, the project manager reviews the list to determine what details best project the nonprofit's desired image. To do this, the manager must know the primary use and purpose of the report. For example, will the annual report be directed to other associations to appeal for funds from a foundation? Or will the report accompany grant requests? A nonprofit can distribute an annual report in con-junction with a fund drive or use it as "a calling card" to introduce itself to a potential donor. A local charity may opt to use this publica-tion to accompany a direct-mail piece to raise supplemental funding to cover emergency expenses.

In the aforementioned instances, the nonprofit focuses on a pri-mary "investor," hoping to persuade the "investor" to contribute to the cause. Still, an annual report is not used exclusively for one audience, but rather has multiple uses. Nevertheless, prioritizing the use of the document and identifying the primary audience is valu-able. For instance, the individual contributor is probably more inter-ested in knowing how much money the agency funneled into the community during the past year; whereas, a foundation may want to know which nonprofit is focusing on a particular educational or social problem.

After identifying the target audience and the primary use of the report, other applications can be considered for this document. Non-profits send annual reports to the press to raise the media's level of awareness about the organizations' work in an effort to gain print space or air time. The report is shared with labor unions, educators, and special interest groups to solicit volunteers. Prospective employees are recruited with such a document. Some vendors even request annual reports to verify financial stability before establishing an account.

In fact, annual reports play a major role in the motivation of donors and would-be donors, according to Milton Murray and Ken Turpen in their 1996 article found in   *Fund Raising Management.* Murray, director emeritus for Philanthropic Service for Institutions at the Seventh-Day Adventist Church World Headquarters, and Turpen, managing director at that same institution, contend this document permits nonprofits to employ techniques, such as describing gift clubs, thanking donors and volunteers, publishing a status report of endowment programs, and instilling competition among giving cate-gories, to show how important contributions and volunteers are to the success of the organization. [4]

Consequently, an annual report carries select material to a specific audience, yet communicates the organization's identity to a wide range of readers. Most important, this well-written document consis-tently projects the image that the nonprofit is a "good investment."

This dimension is critical, as donors want to believe they contribute money wisely, that their money is being spent on a "good" organization that is fiscally sound, and that the agency meets its identified goals.

The list of corporate annual report components is analyzed from the specific nonprofit's perspective. Corporate subsidiary text can be replaced by copy on special programs. Number of employees can be translated into number of clients served by an agency on an annual basis. Grant funding can be recorded in place of a corporation's comment on bonds. In short, all traditional elements are customized to communicate the agency's story.

Care is required so as not to "burden" the reader with extraneous or inappropriate data. Only pertinent financial material belongs in the report. However, up-to-date, audited financial information must be retained on file for review upon request by the public or governmental agencies.

TAKING A STRATEGIC APPROACH

One person must assume the ultimate responsibility for the nonprofit's annual report. This is typically the public relations director. As project manager, the PR person then interviews the executive director to ascertain answers to the following questions. This information establishes the parameters of the finished piece and strategically guides the project:

- What role will the executive director play in the development of the organization's annual report?
- Will volunteers be asked to provide input? If so, who? (e.g., the board president, marketing chair, etc.)
- What is the budget?
- Who is the primary audience?
- What photographs/logos, if any, must appear?
- In what ways will the report be used?
- How many copies are needed?
- When is the distribution date?
- Are there any size and/or design restrictions and/or considerations?

- Is a particular writing style desired?
- What traditional annual report components should be included?

Although answers to these questions serve as a starting point, the budget issue deserves elaboration. Producing an annual report is costly. In fact, the corporate report publishing industry was estimated at $8.4 billion in 1997. [5] In a survey conducted by the National Investor Relations Institute, the average cost per annual report in 1996 was $4.01. [6] In addition, 61 percent of the press runs involved fewer than 50,000 copies. [7] Therefore, this figure reflects a cost per unit press run that differs dramatically from the needs of most nonprofits.

The four major costs in producing an annual report are design, typography, photography, and printing. High cost-per-unit figures may concern the small nonprofit, but it is necessary to possess an awareness of the potential expense when a high-quality annual report is created, especially if only a small quantity is needed.

No one expects a tax-exempt organization to publish an elaborate or expensive annual report. However, an amateurish document can damage the organization's reputation. Therefore, a nonprofit must determine the type of finished product it wants in relationship to its budget. Equipped with this knowledge, a timetable is developed and a decision made regarding the use of hired talent.

Review time is built into the production schedule. This permits adequate review time for the certified public accountant and executive director. Depending upon the size and structure of the association and the formality of the report, a review by an attorney, the association's treasurer, or even a committee of volunteers may be required.

Budget also impacts the scheduling process. For example, a large budget permits the possibility of color photos. If so, time is required for photo taking, the selection process, the incorporation of photographs into the design, lab time for color separations, and extra time on the press. Without photographs, less time and a smaller budget may be adequate for the project.

Deadlines should be cushioned in anticipation of Murphy's Law. A press breaking down, photographs shot a second time, and personnel who must be interviewed or approve copy represent situations that impact schedule dates. If freelance or design agency talent is hired, additional time is needed for the interviewing process. When developing the schedule, it is best to work backward from the planned distribution date. In the corporate world, seven to fifteen months[8] are allotted for annual report planning and production.

With a target distribution date and final budget, the project manager specifies who is assigned to the various tasks and establishes deadlines. A review of the elements listed in Table 2.1 offer insight into the numerous steps involved in the development process.

TABLE 2.1. Annual Report Schedule

Assignment	Person Responsible	Deadline
Select annual report team captain		
Determine the audience and primary use of the report		
Develop the theme of the publication		
Prepare a tentative layout		
Solicit bids from and select a designer, photographer, and printer		
Conduct interviews		
Develop first draft of report		
Obtain approval of first draft		
Obtain approval of tentative financial information from the certified public accountant		
Gather creative elements (shoot photos, sketch illustrations, etc.)		
Finalize selection of creative elements		
Submit final draft of text for approval		
Deliver color transparencies to printer		
Submit type and mechanicals of early closing section to printer		
Prepare late closing sections, including financials		
Submit blue line to review committee for approval		
Proofread printer's copy off of the press		
Give approval to printer for printing		
Distribute the report		

THE DESIGN

Ideally, the project manager locates a design firm to donate its services to prepare the document. A freelance designer or the art school at a local university or community college may also be willing to perform such a service on a pro bono basis. Although such an arrangement is extremely desirable, many charities are not fortunate enough to obtain such a donation.

What does a designer do? The designer establishes the organization's image through the layout of the report, paying attention to the tiniest detail in order to subtly promote the objective of the document without detracting from the written message. If the report has numerous pages, it is well worth the cost to hire professional talent. However, professional assistance is expensive. Sixty-six percent of publicly traded companies rely on outside design support at an annual average cost of $39,000, which includes other tasks such as typesetting and photography. [9] It is advisable to check with local design firms and negotiate a standard per-hour fee or a flat rate that is compatible with the nonprofit's budget constraints.

Some of the functions performed by a report designer are to:

- Organize the material to be used.
- Determine the page size and number of pages.
- Lay out copy in a readable and inviting format.
- Select typeface and type size.
- Establish margins.
- Select photos and mark for cropping.
- Create charts, tables, etc.
- Locate appropriate illustrations.
- Determine number of ink colors.
- Choose paper stock.

If the report is thematically unified, a cohesive document is produced. The thrust of the document must be uncomplicated. This permits the design and text to transmit a single, easy-to-recall message. It is ideal to make this the same message the nonprofit wants communicated throughout the entire year.

According to Sid Cato, who publishes *Newsletter on Annual Reports,* themes are commonly used by the annual reporting industry to tie together design and content. [10] To achieve this, writing and design teams meet from the onset to determine what conceptual approach best conveys the theme and then to translate this through complimentary design and copy. For example, text printed over photos, text reversed out, or too little use of white space makes even the best copy uninviting to read by creating a feeling of closure, clutter, or disorganization.

If the nonprofit adheres to a simple format, freelance talent or an agency may not be required, which keeps production costs low. The budget may even preclude the use of a professional designer. If so, the manager assumes the design task, locates a trained volunteer, or selects the most talented person in-house.

If this task is not performed by a professional, a simple but tasteful and appropriate layout can be created as long as basic rules of good design are followed. Suggestions regarding pertinent components follow.

Length

Corporations produce annual reports of various sizes. In 1996, the average annual report was 46 pages long. [11] This compares to a six-panel report that may provide sufficient narrative and financial coverage for a small nonprofit. [12] Consequently, content impacts the publication's size. With the quantity of material specified, the designer refers to budget limitations and selects the most appropriate graphic elements.

Cover

The cover is the reader's first visual contact with the annual report. Therefore, the cover's importance cannot be overlooked. Color and illustrations frequently are used to attract readers, even if color is not used inside.

According to Sid Cato, "If the company doesn't know enough to make the cover demand that the recipient become a reader, reward it by heaving its report into the nearest receptacle." [13] Strong words but when one considers the number of tax-exempt entities competing for financial and volunteer support, and the volume of print media demanding our attention, this outlook typifies most readers.

An exciting photograph makes a very effective cover as long as it reinforces the organization's image. Faces and body language can project warm and positive feelings. Such an approach is particularly strategic for the nonprofit that serves people rather than causes.

Care must be taken when choosing "models." Options include selecting someone involved with the nonprofit, a readily identifiable individual, or a professional. This decision is based on who can best help accentuate the theme and keep the organization free from any legal problems.

Scenes symbolic of the organization's main activity, the name of the organization, or a news headline format are three other options for the publication's cover. Embossing or foil stamping on richly colored paper is another alternative.

If budget-cutting is required, the number of colors can be limited. Ink must compliment paper color. The wording of the theme, a simple illustration, or the organization's logo usually works well on this type of cover. Of course, if the agency's logo is printed, the logo's integrity must be protected by reproducing the image in the correct ink color.

Color

Budget ultimately dictates the ability to use color inside the report. Use of four-color in an annual report produces an extremely impressive piece. However, the expense of color separations or of printing in several inks may surpass the budget. Also, the danger exists of creating "too slick" of a report, giving the impression that the nonprofit is not efficiently using its funds.

Colors can be limited to those traditionally associated with the organization. Another possibility is to use black ink for printing the text, while using one other color to highlight the design work. The contrasting color must not suggest a meaning other than the one intended. For example, printing financial material in red connotates that the numbers are "in the red," indicating a negative balance.

Paper

The weight, coating, and color of paper are subtle characteristics, which contribute to the overall appearance. Glossy, coated surfaces work extremely well for printing photographs. A second grade of paper is often used for financials. Typically, a nonglossy paper is used for this section to enhance the readability of numbers and statistics and to allow a reader to easily write notes on it. With improvements made in recycled paper, approximately two thirds of today's annual reports contain recycled paper. Some organizations even print their entire report on recycled paper. [14]

The opacity of the paper is equally important. Opacity refers to the capability of the paper to take ink on one side without allowing the print to show through onto the other side. The texture of paper and how its surface works with photographs must be considered as well. Finally, the compatibility of ink and paper colors must be checked.

Two other important factors, not frequently considered by the novice designer, are the weight and size of the paper. If the nonprofit is a major, national organization and intends to mail a large quantity of reports, weight plays a significant role in the initial cost of production as well as in the mailing cost of the finished piece. The Council on Foundations suggests a 65-lb. cover stock for publishing a simple, brochure-style annual report. [15]

Approximately 78 percent of all corporate annual reports are printed in an 8 ½-inch-by-11-inch format. [16] A nonstandard size is used to distinguish the annual report from "tradition," but it is wise to stay within a "file drawer" size. Whether the nonprofit opts to follow tradition or takes a creative approach, paper size is an economic factor to consider. For example, will producing a nontraditional format result in nonstandard paper waste, thereby adding unnecessary cost to the project?

The grain of the paper impacts printability and foldability. The "grain" refers to the direction in which fibers line up on the sheet. It is best to discuss such fine points with a designer or printer early in the process, since the grain can impact the appearance of the finished product as well as the need to have a piece scored prior to folding.

Photographs

Photographs and illustrations were mentioned in conjunction with the front cover. Color and paper choice also influence the reproduction of these art forms. Before any graphic devices reach the reproduction state, determine if photographs, illustrations, or a complimentary combination of both best accentuates the report's theme.

At one time, photographs were considered a frill. Now, they are recognized as a tool to create dramatic emphasis. A study of annual reports commissioned by Potlatch found that if photography or illustration was dropped from a corporate annual report, the publication was likely to disinterest six out of every ten individual investors and portfolio managers. [17] Since charities are looking for "individual investors," it is obvious that photography or illustration is a worthwhile addition.

Including people in photographs adds warmth to the report's tone. It is preferable for shots to be candid, as an informal appearance is typically considered refreshing. Scenes from everyday life create a natural look.

Carefully planned, shot, and cropped, a "photo of reality" visually depicts what words alone cannot portray. However, photographs can suggest more than one meaning, so the photo must be examined from multiple perspectives. All photographs should be selectively reviewed. Only pictures making a maximum contribution should be incorporated into the report.

If persons in photos are recognizable, it is critical for the nonprofit to protect itself legally before publishing the photographs. The person who appears must be contacted and asked to sign a photo permission form (see Forms 2.1 and 2.2).

Forms are either very specific regarding photo usage or generic. When the individual signs the photo permission slip, he or she gives written permission for the organization to use the picture. The form states if the picture is to be used in an exclusive or limited manner or if multiple uses are permitted. It is imperative for the "model" to sign the form and for the form to be retained on file in the public relations department. This precaution deters people from trying to collect money for the photo appearance at a later time. An even better safeguard is to pay a $1 modeling fee in payment for appearance in the picture. Thus, the individual is "officially" paid for time and talent. An excellent public relations idea is to give a copy of the photograph and a copy of the finished publication to the volunteer model who posed.

FORM 2.1. Photo Permission Release Form

(NAME OF NONPROFIT ORGANIZATION)
ANNUAL REPORT PHOTO PERMISSION RELEASE FORM

I, _____, do hereby grant permission to (Name of Nonprofit)
(Please Print Name)

to use my likeness or photographic image and my name in its (year) annual

report. I do hereby limit the use of this photo to this specific publication, (Name

of Publication). It is understood by me and (Name of Nonprofit) that my likeness

and/or image shall be used in a professional and positive manner. This docu-

ment becomes valid once my signature is added to it and a sum of $ _____

is paid to me.

_____   _____   _____
Talent/Model Signature   Social Security Number   Date

_____   _____
Representative of   Date
(Name of Nonprofit)

FORM 2.2. Photo Permission Release Form

(NAME OF NONPROFIT ORGANIZATION)
PROMOTIONAL PHOTO PERMISSION RELEASE FORM

I, _____, do hereby grant permission to (Name of Nonprofit)
　　(Please Print Name)

to use my likeness or photographic image and my name in its promotional,

advertising, and/or internal communication campaigns. I do not limit this use to

conclude at a specific time or date. It is understood by me and (Name of

Nonprofit) that my likeness and/or image shall be used in a professional and

positive manner. This document becomes valid once my signature is added to

it and a sum of $_____ is paid to me.

_____   _____   _____

Talent/Model Signature   Social Security Number   Date

_____   _____

Representative of   Date
(Name of Nonprofit)

"People shots" can be acquired by two other means. Certain companies sell stock photographs by catalog. When purchasing this type of photo, the rights for the particular use are bought. It is not uncommon for purchasers to request exclusive usage from the supplier within the specific market niche. For example, if a hospital purchased a stock photo for in its annual report, a request for exclusivity in the industry is made, preventing the vendor from letting another hospital use the picture in its annual report.

The other option is to hire a professional model. Depending upon the notoriety and charitableness of this person, a wide range of fees could be charged for securing such a photo.

Photo selection is influenced by the plan to print in full color, spot color, or black and white. In the past, black and white was considered the "bottom of the visual totem pole," frequently connoting old, cheap, dull, and quiet. However, black and white has experienced a renaissance. Black and white photography is now appreciated for its unique emotional appeal. Of course, the ability to visually communicate through black and white pictures versus the use of costly four-color photographs affects production price.

Duotones offer yet another possibility. A duotone is a photograph printed in two colors. In some situations, a designer recommends printing a photo in black with a second color used in specific locations on the print. This creative method differentiates a report by giving it a nontraditional appeal. Another example of a duotone is printing a photograph in black and a sepia tone. This produces an old-time appearance. Even though both examples use only two colors of ink to reproduce the photo, duotones obviously offer a creative flair.

What cost is associated with annual report photography? "Expensive" is very likely the answer. Day rate estimates for a professional photographer range from $500 to $3,000 per day with topflight individuals commanding the higher salaries. If travel is required, it is the nonprofit's responsibility to cover this expense as well. The photographer's travel time also may be billed at half of the regular day shooting rate. In some cases, a photographer's assistant, who helps set up complex shots, is required. Of course, the assistant receives a fee as well.

These aforementioned costs simply cover time and talent. Film and processing are not included in these fees.

When studying portfolios, the photographer's forte must be considered. Typically, photographers have specialties, such as on-location shots or people photos. Use of a single photographer minimizes the range of artistic interpretation and ensures continuity in perspective. On the other hand, photography required on an international scale may make the thought of hiring more than one photographer appealing. Budget constraints, the quality of all photography, and the ability to find photographers with compatible styles all play a role in this decision.

Recognizing the limited budget of most nonprofits, the portfolios of newer photographers should be considered, as this talent is normally purchased at an economical rate. Ideally, a photographer donates his or her talent to the nonprofit.

One issue to discuss is photo ownership rights. Professional photographers own these rights unless previously discussed and a different agreement is reached. If possible, nonprofits should obtain the rights to all pictures during the negotiation process. This allows the nonprofit to use the photos later without incurring added expense.

After hiring a photographer, the annual report manager familiarizes this individual with the theme, goals, and design concept of the report. With this background, the photographer creates the best visual images possible through the camera lens.

Illustrations

An illustration is a sketch or line drawing that offers a creative, effective, and flexible way to visually communicate the report's theme. Illustrations offer a graphic alternative to photographs, setting them apart from the rest of the report and creating a visual that demands increased attention.

Frequently, illustrations convey an intangible or abstract concept better than a photograph. Illustrations can also emphasize certain attributes better than photographs. Plus, minute details, not easily seen in a photograph, can be accentuated in a sketch.

An illustration serves as a break from photos, creating a visual change of pace. Hence, an illustration becomes a welcome addition to a report filled with photography. It is best to use original art or to have a print that meets camera-ready specifications to ensure quality reproduction.

The use of a photograph or an illustration also involves a marketing implication. If the photograph or sketch embodies the feeling of the organization, the nonprofit should consider enlarging it and making copies. The print or photograph can be signed by the photographer, illustrator, or model, and distributed to key donors as limited edition items. The art can even be made into a poster to help carry the nonprofit's message to the public. Thus, multiple uses make a photograph or an illustration a cost-effective investment.

Another artistic device to consider is pastiche. A modern version of the popular collage of the 1960s, it combines various images into one work to convey a message or theme.

Graphic Devices

Graphic devices aid reader comprehension. Charts, tables, graphs, and diagrams make confusing financial or statistical information easier to understand. Tables and graphs readily display relationships between ideas and physical properties in a concise format. As a result, well-designed graphics save time for busy readers.

Graphic aids increase the likelihood of the report being read, since the document becomes visually inviting. The eye is drawn toward graphic aids. Important material otherwise overlooked can be highlighted in a chart or graph. If tastefully and artistically executed, graphic aids can even build reader confidence by lending a sense of authority to the document. Consequently, time and money should be spent on developing these visuals to make the report appealing.

It is not always easy to determine which graphic aids ensure design appeal and maximize readership comprehension. Therefore, it is best to have a working knowledge of all options and a solid understanding of how these visual aids are best used. A few hints regarding the use of graphic aids are:

- Resist the temptation to reduce graphics just so they can be placed on one page.
- Clearly know what your message is and what type of comparison you are trying to accomplish.

- Be sure to locate the graphic device near the text it helps to explain.
- Round off numbers, if appropriate, so the message of the graphic is not complicated.
- Each graphic should carry a title and caption.
- Neatness is imperative.
- Use of rules and borders will help display the data.

The visual aids typically found in an annual report are line or mountain charts, bar graphs, pictograms, pie charts, and tables. A discussion of the various visuals follows.

Line Charts

Line charts are widely understood and considered superior to bar graphs for their ability to exhibit a trend or ongoing series of changes. Time is customarily charted on the horizontal or x-axis. Quantitative measures, such as monetary units, are usually plotted on the vertical or y-axis.

Captions, legends, and grid lines must be sufficiently labeled, so information is clearly and accurately represented. This is particularly true with multiple-line charts, where two or more lines are plotted on a single grid. The multiple-line chart compares two or more types of data. Such a mechanism is extremely useful in displaying trends or cycles.

Two other factors contribute to the frequent use of this particular graphic: ease of development and low production cost. Simple line charts are adequately printed in one color. If multiple lines are used, extra colors or different "lines," such as dashed or solid, make the chart easier to read. The actual preparation of a line chart is relatively easy.

If displaying a single line, the information is printed in a line that is thicker than the vertical or horizontal scale lines that shape the grid (see Figure 2.1). Two variations of the simple line chart permit this visual to communicate comparative information. A grouped line chart enables multiple lines to be positioned on the grid, using contrasting colors, line widths, or patterns. The challenge is to determine how many lines are too many (see Figure 2.2). A surface chart is created by coloring or shading the surface between the trend and base lines   (see Figure 2.3).[18]

FIGURE 2.1. Sample of a Single-Line Chart

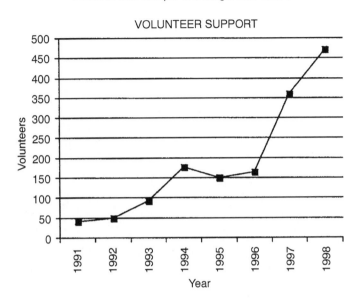

FIGURE 2.2. Sample of a Grouped Line Chart

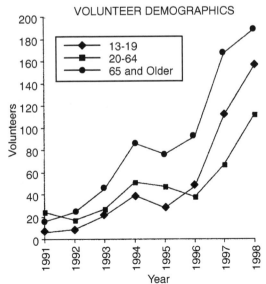

FIGURE 2.3. Sample of a Surface Chart

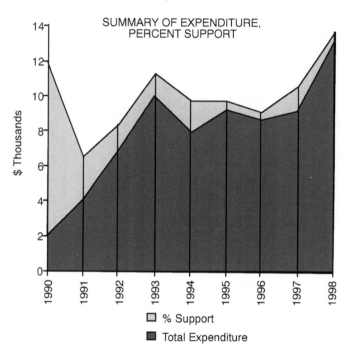

Bar Graphs

A bar graph consists of one or more horizontal or vertical bars superimposed on a background grid. The grid is arithmetically scaled, so the length or height of each bar displays a quantitative value in a particular category. Usually, the scale starts at "0" to aid reader comprehension. Scale values and captions as well as the title of the bar graph should be accurately and clearly labeled. In a financial statement, all titles should be centered with an identical font heading.

The simple bar graph is used the most frequently of any bar graph, because it is easy to understand (see Figure 2.4). A multiple bar graph displays the quantitative value of two or more sets of variables within the same exhibit (see Figure 2.5). The plus or

FIGURE 2.4. Sample of a Bar Graph

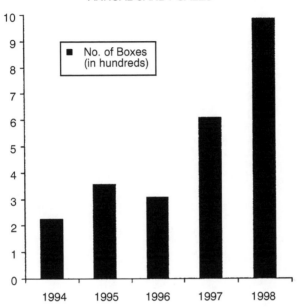

ANNUAL CANDY SALES

minus deviation bar is excellent for reflecting percentages or exhibiting changes.

In a truncated bar graph, the height or length of each bar is shortened by removing an equal size segment. This reduces the size of the chart. Although convenient, this graph may be misread by the hurried reader, resulting in misconception.

Subdivided bar graphs present comparisons of data within each bar. Varying degrees of shading or hatching are used, if the graph is printed in one color. Otherwise, multiple colors define the various factors represented in each bar. If several components are involved or if the height or length of the bars measures 100 percent, the subdivided bar graph becomes very difficult to read.

When creating a bar graph, select the color with the greatest contrast or shading to emphasize the most important item. Compo-

FIGURE 2.5. Sample of a Multiple Bar Graph

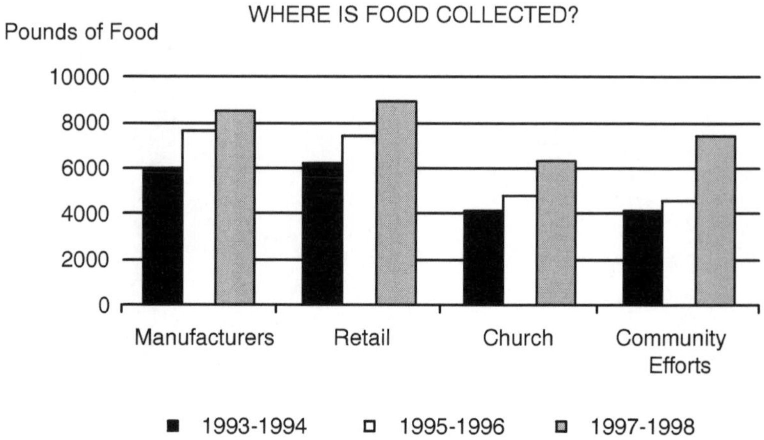
WHERE IS FOOD COLLECTED?
Pounds of Food
10000
8000
6000
4000
2000
0
Manufacturers
Retail
Church
Community Efforts
1993-1994
1995-1996
1997-1998

nent order is selected based on what best serves the communication process.[19]

Pictograms

A pictogram uses highly simplified visual representations of objects or qualities to depict a story or meaning in order to communicate statistical data. For example, Christmas trees may be used to demonstrate the results of an annual fund raiser or houses to demonstrate number of households signed up for a particular program.

The problem with pictograms is that the chosen symbols may be unclear to the reader. Thus, the wrong topic or meaning can be connoted. (See Figure 2.6.)

Charts

The organizational chart is frequently used in an annual report. This chart reveals the hierarchical structure of the organization in descending order of importance or function. Each position is labeled and often enclosed in a box. Titles are brief and precise. This

FIGURE 2.6. Sample of a Pictogram

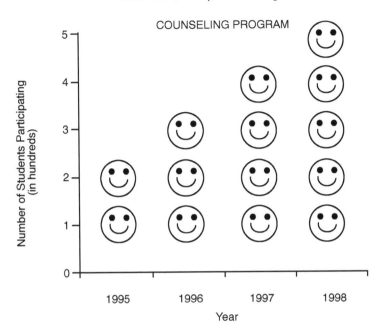

ensures accurate representation of the organization's system. Management and line positions are portrayed by this graphic aid.   (See Figure 2.7.)

Flow charts are powerful tools used to explain the step-by-step process of an activity. Usually, boxes are labeled and connected by arrows to demonstrate the interrelationship among the various steps. (See Figure 2.8.)

A pie chart is a useful device to display component comparison, especially when not more than six items are involved.   [20] This visual is similar to a subdivided graph in that the sum of the individual components is depicted as creating the whole. Each component is a slice or wedge of the circle. The largest value is often drawn in the first wedge, beginning at the 12 o'clock position. The components then are placed in descending order around the circle. If a number of tiny components are included, these are usually grouped into a

FIGURE 2.7. Sample of an Organizational Chart

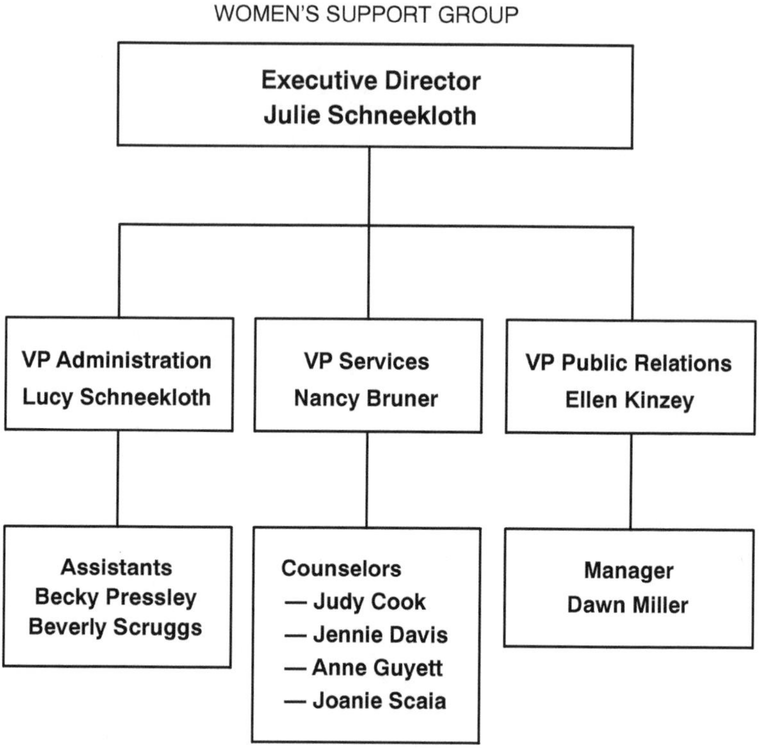

WOMEN'S SUPPORT GROUP

miscellaneous or "other" category. To emphasize certain information, a wedge can be "lifted" out of the pie.

Color, shading, or patterns are used to differentiate the slices
within the pie chart. If this is done, a legend accompanies the chart,
so the coded sections are defined.   (See Figure 2.9.)

Maps

Maps are used to display geographical distribution, scope, or
relationship such as distance, distribution, or community boundaries. If used in an annual report, subareas should be captioned or
numbered, so the reader understands the relationship the map has to
the report. (See Figure 2.10.)

FIGURE 2.8. Sample of a Flow Chart

ANNUAL REPORT APPROVAL PROCESS

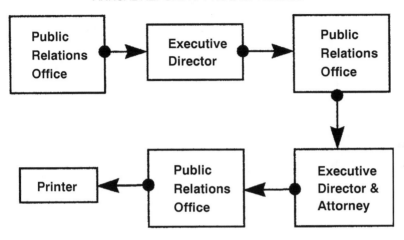

FIGURE 2.9. Sample of a Pie Chart

1998 FUNDING SOURCES

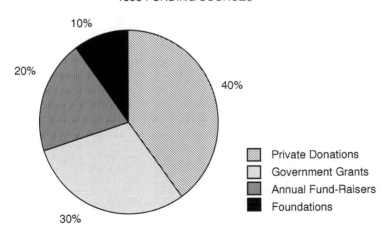

FIGURE 2.10. Sample of a Map

HEALTH CARE OPERATIONS

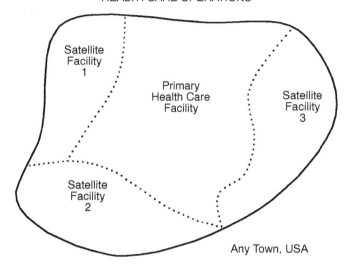

Any Town, USA

Tables

Tables are used to help the reader understand complex relationships more easily. If two or more columns are used, delineating captions should be placed over each column. If tables contain titles and sub-headings, they should be boxed with horizontal lines. Thus, the body of the data is separated from the titles. (See Table 2.2.)

TABLE 2.2. Sample of a Table

1998 PROGRAM PARTICIPATION

City	Potential	Teens Served	Penetration Rate One in . . .
Fairview	7,244	768	9.4
Mount Center	4,286	631	7.1
Cedar Fields	15,434	2,394	6.5
Plain View	52,402	7,893	6.0

Type

The typography selected for an annual report makes the difference between creating a document with a raw amateur look or projecting a polished, quality image. In an annual report, type should not be printed smaller than 8 point. In fact, 10 or 12 point proves to be a greater "comfort zone" for the reader. Remember the audience reading this document. If the nonprofit is targeting an older demographic base, common sense dictates the use of a larger point size. Statistical information becomes very difficult to read when reduced, so readability based on point size is particularly important in this section, too.

Headline and display type act as important graphic elements, because both help to convey the impression of the report. A variance in type also sets off main sections of the text, making it easier for a reader to locate particular topics within the copy.

Five factors must be considered when selecting type. First, what typeface will look best? At this point, a decision is made between a serif or sans serif style. In the following example, appearance is clearly impacted:

Times New Roman is an example of a serif type. Notice the little "flags" on each letter.

This is News Gothic typeface. Notice the clean lines without the addition of flags.

Serif type is considered easier to read, because the "flags" connect the type, leading the eye from one letter to the next.

Second, the weight of the type must be considered. What looks best in which segment of the report? Light, medium, demi-bold, and bold are a few of the options.

This is Rockwell Condensed type. Notice how closely the letters are spaced.

This Rockwell typeface is printed in bold.

This type is Rockwell Light. Notice the difference in letter weight.

Third, style plays a role in obtaining the desired look in the allotted space. For example, is condensed or wide type more appropriate? Would photo captions look better in italic or Roman?

This Courier New type is printed in italic.

This is the same typeface but without the italic look.

Fourth, spacing between the lines of type, referred to as leading, influences the appearance and the readability of the text. Consequently, thought must go into how this factor impacts the appearance of the document. Also up for consideration is the issue of using upper case, lower case, or a combination of both.

Finally, type is set in a justified, unjustified   (also known as ragged), or centered format. If type is justified, all lines of copy are the same length, and they align on the right and left margins. Unjustified type is aligned on the left side of the line with a ragged right. Copy that is centered uses a central point from which letters are equally distributed, creating both ragged right and left sides.

It is best to break the copy into two or three columns per page. Even though a single column or four columns per page is acceptable, annual reports traditionally use a two- or three-column format. A wider column is difficult to read. Type must always be selected and arranged, based on legibility, aesthetics, and volume of copy for the allotted space.

After the text is formatted on the computer, the project manager checks the laser prints. This step helps to locate errors prior to the expensive blueline stage. With today's computer technology, laser prints are easy to output, so the nonprofit should take advantage of this by incorporating sufficient checks into the process.

Additional cost savings materialize if the nonprofit has a computer that is compatible with the one used by the typesetter. The nonprofit can prepare text on the agency's computer and submit discs or electronically transmit the material to the typesetter. Not having to directly enter the text into the computer—a time saving result—reduces typesetting costs.

For-profit corporations set an extensive amount of type. The average cost of typesetting an annual report for a publicly traded company is $11,379. [21] Of course, most nonprofits would not communicate this same volume of data.

White Space

Although white space does not usually come to mind when thinking of design techniques, it plays a major role in layout. Properly used, white space projects an image of elegance and quality. White space also makes an element stand out on a page, because the area surrounding it is not crowded. However, care is necessary to avoid arbitrarily trapped space in the design just because no copy or graphic fills the void. If trapped white space occurs, a very unappealing look results.

Binding

Smaller annual reports can be folded to the desired size, if only one sheet of paper is required. As a report becomes more complex with multiple pages, binding is required. Binding options include saddle stitch, side-wire bound, mechanical binding, edition, and perfect binding.

Saddle stitch is the most common method used for a booklet or pamphlet. The booklet is opened and wires (staples) are inserted through the backbone. Then, the three sides are trimmed. This is a relatively inexpensive method of binding.

With side-wire stitching, wires are inserted one-fourth inch from the edge of the binding, passing from front to back. The wires are cinched close, and the spine taped. This technique works well for thicker books but does not project as professional an appearance as some of the binding options available.

To hold cover pages together by mechanical means, holes are drilled and plastic or wire coils are inserted. Thus, the finished product has the appearance of a notebook or spiral tablet. All four sides of the booklet are trimmed before holes are drilled rather than after.

Edition binding is also referred to as "casebound" or "hard cover." It is the most expensive and permanent form of binding. The pages are sewn together and then glue is added to the spine to reinforce the stitching.

Use of perfect binding is increasing the most quickly of any form of binding. Pages and cover are held together with an adhesive. After the cover is glued to the spine of the book, the cover and pages are trimmed as a unit. The publication must be at least thirty pages for this technique to work.

A Graphic Summary

For a quality design, each element must be analyzed. What contribution does it make to the overall appearance of the document? How well does the element work with other design factors? The following list contains key design points:

1. Do not interfere with the presentation of information in an annual report by using a design that detracts from the data.
2. Use tables, graphs, pie charts, and other aids to more effectively communicate statistical information.
3. Take advantage of the trend to use black and white photography. It helps control production costs.
4. Combine appropriate sections to reduce unnecessary pages and costs.
5. Reuse good photos by recropping to give a fresh appearance without incurring the expense involved with new photography.
6. Be sure to obtain written permission from the source when reproducing copyrighted phraseology or graphic aids. Keep this written approval in your records.
7. Utilize wide columns and leading to make reading easier.
8. Obtain bids for all aspects of design and production to assure the job can be completed before encountering budget problems. Receive updated quotes when design changes are made.
9. Be sure to use well-focused photography and clean art.
10. Limit illustrations to one page and place the illustration facing the text it supports.

11. Move a particularly large chart or table to the appendix, especially if it clutters the look of the page design.
12. Lay out each page so financial information is integrated into the design of the entire book.
13. Resist the temptation to use a graphic aid if a sentence can communicate the material more effectively.
14. Number tables and figures by the Arabic system (1,2,3,4) if several graphic aids are used. To identify only a few graphic devices, Roman numerals can be used.
15. Use photo and chart caption. Headline pages or sections.
16. Proofread, proofread, proofread! The earlier an error is discovered in the process, the less costly it is to correct.
17. Correct errors if they are located prior to printing. If the report is published before an error is found, the significance of the error must be considered relative to the cost of a second printing and possible late distribution.

What design trends are seen in today's corporate reporting? In corporate annual reports, graphs and charts are common visual aids. Photographs are frequently used. Margin call-outs in body copy are a third choice, followed by illustrations. [22] As already stated, 8½-by-11-inch format is a popular size. Perfect binding and saddle stitch rank first and second as the preferred methods for binding. A greater environmental sensitivity is recognized, with more companies utilizing recycled paper. [23] As more companies have global operations, some corporations are printing their reports in several languages. [24]

Should these design trends be followed by nonprofits? That question is not easily answered. A nonprofit must be extremely aware of its primary audience and how the annual report will be perceived. A professional but not extravagant image is the look a nonprofit should strive to project through its annual report, and design plays a major role in creating this image.

For example, an annual report published on recycled paper would complement the image of an environmental group. A bilingual report, rather than one written solely in English, would better serve nonprofits located in certain parts of the United States. Carefully designed graphics printed in one color of ink on colored paper stock may be sufficient for the small agency. The large, national nonprofit must project a frugal image yet publish a report with a professional appearance. A better grade of paper, photographs, or similar features may be used to upgrade a report. Consequently, a creative approach within the confines of the agency's budget serves as the guiding principle in annual report design.

THE CONTENT

An attractive annual report entices readers to pick up the publication and begin reviewing it. But the document must have substance. It must contain pertinent information that is of interest to readers. Publicly traded companies are required to divulge extensive financial information, to explain why a setback has occurred, and to substantiate a firm's accomplishments. In effect, the annual report of a corporation is a year-long business record measuring the company's effort in dollars and dividends.

Nonprofit organizations should offer adequate financial information in their reports as testimony to the association's fiscal responsibility and efficient service to its membership. What happened during the past year, why it happened, the known or anticipated effects, and how the organization fits into the community are other possible topics for an annual report. Simply stated, the nonprofit must select copy and statistical data to justify its existence to the community and its investors.

In the report opening, the nonprofit should prepare a statement or paragraph defining its purpose and identifying the organization, much as a corporation does in its business description. A table of contents shows what is in the report and provides a point of reference for the reader. It even can include a brief description or quote from the text, sometimes called a "talking table of contents." Of course, a table of contents is not necessary in a small annual report.

The financial highlights in a corporate annual report are designed to meet the requirements of the Securities and Exchange Act of 1934 and the 1980 amendments. This regulation states that publicly traded companies must provide annual reports to stockholders at least fifteen days prior to the corporation's annual meeting. Financial data spanning the most recent five-year time frame, a certified financial statement for the previous two years, an expanded discussion and analysis of the company's financial condition, an explanation of any discrepancies between these statements and those filed with the SEC, identification of company directors' principal occupations, plus stock market and dividend information for the past two years are required. [25]

The nonprofit can carefully select pertinent statistical content without providing such detail. A consolidated balance sheet and income statement may be in order. The balance sheet outlines the assets and liabilities of the organization. A statement regarding the agency's funding sources can help readers understand how operational funds were raised. Although unnecessary, an auditor's opinion, which indicates that an independent certified public accountant reviewed the financial statement and that it is correct and in accordance with general accounting standards, is a strong addition to the financial section.

The Letter

The letter from the president and/or executive director is an excellent addition to any size annual report and should occupy a prominent spot. In a survey conducted by Yankelovich Partners for Potlatch Corporation, the chairman's letter to the shareholders was ranked as 5.6 on a 6-point scale in terms of importance. [26] In fact, the corporate project manager usually spends more time on this particular creative component than on any other element within the annual report. [27]

As in the for-profit environment, the nonprofit's executive director initiates the ideas for the letter. A number of topics are appropriate for this section of the report: professional development of staff and volunteers, anticipated issues, reorganization, highlights of the year, projections and future activities of the agency, short-term goals and strategies, and an explanation of how the organization is dealing with a crisis. If political or economic matters need to be discussed or if delicate policy issues must be explained, this letter is an avenue into discussion of such topics.

This is the only signed segment of the annual report, other than the auditor's opinion. It is advisable to have the chief executive officer draft the letter, so the leader's vision, intelligence, and passion for the organization are conveyed. Therefore, readers can better understand those managing the nonprofit and gain insight into the organization.

The public relations writer reviews the officer's draft and makes suggestions. Brevity is the key to maximizing readership. The letter must also be honest and forthright, without being an executive soapbox. Subheads can also be added to the letter to enhance readability. The synergy of the executive and public relations departments produces a well-written and highly effective letter.

The letter is always signed by the president or executive director. Names are also typed and accompanied by titles. The letter is dated with the day the manuscript is sent to the printer.

Descriptive Information

The document includes "basics" such as the complete name of the organization, the address of its headquarters and other appropriate real estate, the name of the agency director, and a map depicting geographical service boundaries or a description of these boundaries.

A list of board member names is a necessity. The amount of accompanying data usually is tied to available space and personal preference. Organizational board titles, such as secretary or member-at-large, are important. Length of service on the board, year the present term ends, and the individual's position within the community or the person's full-time job are possible elements for inclusion but are not required.

Just as corporate annual reports place key management in the forefront, it is advisable to identify officers and key employees. An organizational chart or a roster of names and corresponding titles works effectively to communicate this information.

The Narrative

A narrative educates the reader on the purpose of the organization and highlights achievements or unusual events, such as the organization's centennial or a move to new headquarters. Nonprofits can use the annual report as a recognition piece, too. The names of major benefactors, special contributors, and volunteers can be incorporated into the report. Often, corporate annual reports pay tribute to employees, and nonprofits can easily do the same. Management should be presented in the best possible light, promoting a successful team concept. Staff recognition and accomplishments are possible topics for discussion as well.

Of course, all of this recognition demonstrates that individuals are as important to the organization as fiscal responsibility. Plus, it makes volunteers view their contributions with additional pride because of the importance the organization obviously places on their efforts.

Other appropriate topics for annual report coverage are special features; comments on equipment and procedures; a description of social action programs; a stand on economic issues; territorial or program expansion; research and development, new marketing, advertising, or public relations information; newly constructed facilities; case histories or success stories; a discussion of industry or community trends; and reaction to these; a comparison to industry standards; and a question-and-answer section.

Topics selected for the annual report must be timely and support the intended image. It is also paramount that the report not appear shallow or lack intrinsic data, regardless of the production budget or the primary audience. The only way to determine what subjects belong in this section is to conduct extensive research. The public relations staff member crafting the narrative must be thoroughly familiar with the organization and conduct research outside of the nonprofit to have a clear understanding as to how this nonprofit functions within the community and competitive environment.

The Style

Traditionally, annual report writing was analytical in nature. But, the future of annual reporting is to produce a document that integrates financial, editorial, and design components into one work, communicating a single, unified, strategic message with sufficient depth and adequate detail to satisfy a diverse audience. To accomplish this, it is important to remember that an annual report is a form of organizational writing. Organizational writing has three basic purposes: to inform, to request or persuade, and to build goodwill.

Therefore, the nonprofit annual report should be written to inform readers of the nonprofit's status, persuade readers of the value of the organization, and build goodwill.

The nonprofit annual report must be as "reader friendly" as possible. Technical terminology should be avoided. Complex financial terms should be eliminated. If financial terminology is required, a glossary of these terms should be included. Language must be concise and understandable rather than written in a legalistic fashion. Simplicity should be a goal, remembering that even today's corporate annual reports are written for the untrained and nontechnical person.

Use of colorful phrases, action verbs, and exciting adjectives keep the narrative flowing and retain reader interest. This writing style takes skillful crafting but is necessary to retain the attention of most readers.

Since the passage of the Civil Rights Act of 1964, corporations increasingly have become aware of the need to monitor corporate practices for discrimination in the workplace and in written communication, such as an annual report. Similarly, nonprofits must be cognizant of the subliminal message sent if stereotypical words or phrases appear in this document.

Should the tone of the report be formal or informal, conservative or progressive, quiet or aggressive? The writing style must be compatible with the tone communicated through the design, artwork, photography, color, style of type, and subject matter.

Humanizing an annual report is particularly important to a nonprofit. A writing technique that produces this effect is use of "second person." "You" is personal, subjective, and reflects warmth. A conversational style is also established by discussing "your benefits," "your organization," or "your volunteerism." The "you" approach can even be incorporated into the letter from the president, shifting from the impersonal "to whom it may concern" mentality. This helps the reader relate to the nonprofit on a personal level.

To ensure a well-written annual report, the project manager should ask these questions while reviewing the copy:

• Would people who look at this annual report feel good about our nonprofit?

- Would the reader want to offer financial support to the agency?
- Would the reader feel good about volunteering time to the group?

The question-and-answer format should not be overlooked. This style has three advantages over traditional copy. First, a question-and-answer arrangement allows the reader to move quickly to the important points in the text. Second, it is easy to skim, because the questions act as subheads within paragraph copy. Finally, the human element of the organization is imparted to the reader through the personality of the key executive. Although the question-and-answer technique is too lengthy for the small report, it is an alternative method for imparting information while retaining readership.

Whether the annual report takes the form of straight copy, question-and-answer, or a letter with statistical information, the document should be divided into sections. Interesting material should be organized into accessible sections with a liberal use of meaningful headings.

Finally, the writing style contributes significantly to the reader's "feel" for the organization. Active voice has greater credibility than passive voice. Is copy written in a hard-hitting manner? Does the style blend with the image that is projected through the graphic design? If so, a cohesive document stressing a single theme will represent the agency.

WORKING WITH THE PRINTER

By the time the annual report goes to the printer, there should be no surprises. Those who give final approval for publication have reviewed the document's progress throughout the project. Final copy and design approval should be a formality.

Whether the nonprofit uses a local printer or a printing company specializing in financial reports, it should solicit bids. The designer may handle this step. Otherwise, it is advisable to obtain input from the designer, as this individual probably knows the firms with the best performance for the money. If the project manager handles this task, negotiating advice may be available from the designer.

The print bidding process should occur early in the planning process. The bid can be based on previous annual reports. If past annual reports are unavailable or if major design changes are anticipated, a printer relies on printing specifications to project the job cost. The following information must be provided:

- Type of electronic file (program).
- Number of pages.
- Format size.
- Quantity of reports.
- Paper and cover stock.
- Number of ink colors.
- Photography (number and size of photos, black and white or color, etc.).
- Art (camera-ready or on diskette).
- Method of binding.
- Embossing or stamping.
- Lamination.
- Varnishing.
- Number of blueline proofs required.
- Expected delivery date.

The time required to print the annual report should be discussed as well. After design and copy are approved, only a few production days may be required for the printing process to be completed. However, a full-size, high-end annual report could take as many as fifteen days, even with today's technology. Consequently, the number of copies and the sophistication of the job dictate the length of time necessary for this step.

When selecting an annual report printer, there are two types from which to choose: financial and commercial. Financial printers generally have a good grasp of the legal requirements involved in printing fiscal materials for publicly traded corporations. Familiarity with Securities and Exchange Commission guidelines is a definite advantage to look for when a corporation selects its annual report printer. However, it is likely that a local, commercial printer can more adequately serve the nonprofit's annual report printing needs.

Please note that it is a routine and ethical practice for a printer to deliver up to 10 percent more or less than what is stated in the contract. This is in accordance with the *Graphic Communication Business Practices* as adopted by the National Association of Printers and Lithographers. Most good printers have 5 percent or less discrepancy from the quantity stated in the contract. The bill reflects the actual number of print pieces delivered.

Although it is tempting to select the low cost bidder, consider more than price. Poor quality printing affects the image projected by this printed piece. It is a good idea to contact businesses that contract with the printer, as these companies are familiar with the quality of work produced by the printer. Samples of the printing company's work should also be reviewed.

Once a printing firm is selected, it is necessary to supervise the progress of the report through the shop. The printer's tasks include platemaking, printing each side of the press sheet, binding, trimming, and shipping. In some cases, financial printers assist with the proofing process.

Close contact with the printing firm must be maintained throughout the process. This provides an opportunity to review the blueline as well as hand-stapled copies from press sheets.

What is a blueline, and why it is so important to the annual report printing process? Bluelines have many names. They may be called a dylux, position proof, or even a blueprint. However, "blueline" is the most commonly used term. A blueline is created through a photographic process and is labor intensive, which is why the cost of a blueline is expensive. Although reviewing the blueline and making corrections increase production time and cost, it is well worth the price in order to avoid reprinting the report because of a major error.

The blueline is created from the final film from which printing plates are made. The exact dimensions of the document, fold locations, type, and imagery are noted. Since this is the last time the project manager or designer sees the creation of the electronic file produced by the printer, extreme care must be taken to proofread and inspect every aspect of the report. When reviewing the proof, a minor error may be uncovered. Based on budget, a nonprofit may select to ignore slightly broken type or an inconsistent comma. Missing copies or a photograph printed backward would make the report unacceptable. So if a critical flaw is uncovered prior to printing, the problem must be corrected. Obviously, cost is incurred and time is added to the project, but such errors preclude the finished piece from being effective and impact the "image" of the nonprofit.

With advancements in technology, it is important to note that some bluelines are fully digitized. This means that the film stage is deleted. The file goes directly to the printing plate. This makes it even more important to carefully review the laser copies as well as to preview what is shown on the computer screen.

What key areas should be checked?

- Is the size of the document correct?
- Are all the pages included, and are they in the correct sequence?
- Are any elements missing such as type, page number, or art?
- Are there any errors in the financial material? Are dollar signs ($) aligned?
- Are photos properly placed?
- Are charts, tables, and other graphic devices accurately reflected?
- Are there any typographical errors not previously noticed?
- Is the type size correct? Is the type clean and crisp, or is the type broken?
- Do the headlines and text appear in the correct places and line up properly on the page?
- Is the alignment of each page correct?
- Can the report be trimmed and folded in the proper locations?
- Are there any scratches or spots (known as "trash") in the type, art, or solid areas? [28]

In a way, the blueline serves as a "contract" between the nonprofit and the printer, as the nonprofit is required to "sign off" that everything is satisfactory and ready to print. If an error is found later, and the project manager signed the blueline, the printer is not liable for the error. If an error occurs during the press run, and the nonprofit has proof of a printer error, the printer must make cost adjustments or reprint, as appropriate.

When a particularly large job is run or an elaborate report is on the press, it is advisable for the project manager or designer to be on site to spot-check quality. If press checks are desired, it is best to notify the printer during the bidding process. Stopping the presses or delaying the printing process, unless it is the printer's fault, involves added cost.

DISTRIBUTION

Distribution is the next step. Clients and volunteers of the non-profit, the group's board of directors, major contributors, local libraries, select governmental officials, foundations, and representatives of the media should be on the mailing list. If the agency is affiliated with a national association, a complimentary copy should be forwarded to headquarters.

If the report is sent to a large group, such as a college's alumni and contributors, a mailing house may be used. A large mailing house might ship 20,000 to 25,000 annual reports a day. However, handwork, added material, and other factors contribute to the time needed for this process. The vendor will be able to determine the amount of time required for the specific job. In a small agency, the clerical staff might prepare the mailing.

It is also a good idea to print extra annual reports. These can be used throughout the year in capital campaigns or annual fund-raising events, to accompany grant proposals, and to give to the public upon request.

TECHNOLOGY AND ANNUAL REPORTS

Corporate annual reports are appearing on the Web with increasing frequency. The annual report is ranked second among investor communication tools linked to corporate Web sites, second only to news releases, according to Inc. Design. The design firm, headquartered in New York, also reports that approximately seven out of every ten 1996 printed annual reports contained information steering investors toward corporate Web site addresses. [29]

Some financial printers, already sensitive to the growing corporate Internet needs, change annual report print files into floppy disc or CD-ROM formats for storybooks, EDGARIZE files to comply with SEC Web requirements, or digitize material for the World Wide Web.

The trend to produce CD-ROM annual reports is likely to continue. For example, First Union, headquartered in Charlotte, North Carolina, produced its 1997 annual report CD-ROM for about $.75 per disc. Its print version cost approximately $2.25 a copy. [30] Such a cost-saving makes this format worthy of consideration.

When the National Investor Relations Institute surveyed its members, the organization discovered that approximately 10 percent of publicly traded companies used CD-ROM discs or on-line services to increase annual report exposure. [31] Nevertheless, this technology will most likely not fully replace the printed annual report. Even with the advancement of electronic publishing, annual report experts agree that the printed annual report will not be replaced by an on-line version. [32] However, nonprofits should take note. As more nonprofits develop home pages on the Web, it makes sense to translate the print annual report into an interactive format providing another outlet for this useful information.

Chapter 3

Newsletters

Many nonprofits rely on newsletters as an important public relations vehicle. With the advent of desktop publishing, creating this communications tool is much easier than in the past. Many software programs simplify in-house newsletter publication, and books discuss this process in depth. Consequently, the purpose of this chapter is not to substitute for either of these. Instead, this chapter examines various aspects of newsletter publication and analyzes specific elements within the context of the nonprofit realm. These helpful tips and suggestions should further simplify the task of producing a newsletter that has strategic public relations and marketing value for the nonprofit.

A WORD ABOUT DESKTOP PUBLISHING

What is "desktop publishing"? Despite the use of the term "publishing," this effort does not address all components of the publishing process. Desktop publishing makes the tasks of writing, editing, and laying out a publication easier by using computer hardware and specialized software.

Prior to the appearance of word-processing programs, it was difficult to move blocks of copy, delete and add text, and exchange information between writers and editors. In the past, a compositor set type and adjusted the leading between the lines and the kerning of the space between the letters. Then, copy and art went through paste-up. In short, publishing a newsletter the old-fashioned way involved several people and was labor intensive. Now, a single person can perform these assignments with today's sophisticated computer technology, saving time and money.

Desktop publishing emerged in the mid-1980s when Aldus, Adobe, and Apple worked together to create design software, printing software, and font management abilities that pioneered the electronic publishing field. Adobe's contribution was PostScript, a high-resolution software program. In 1984, Paul Brainard created Aldus PageMaker. This program combined functions of low-cost microcomputers and laser printers to produce camera-ready mechanicals for publishing. Brainard actually coined the term "desktop" because the software program, PageMaker, combined writing, editing, designing, and production into a manageable desktop operation. Brainard did not view this technological revelation as eliminating the need for skilled professionals. He simply saw it as another tool for designers. [1]

Adobe and Aldus merged their technology. But for desktop publishing to become a reality, one component was still missing. Apple Computer, Inc. provided the link. Apple became instrumental in the introduction of desktop publishing through its improvement of font management capabilities. Apple claimed its user-friendly desktop-publishing software could produce a sixteen-page newsletter in eight hours rather than the twenty-six hours traditionally required to complete the tasks of typesetting, proofreading, corrections, camera work, and paste-up. In fact, the company marketed the publishing system by claiming it could pay for itself within six months. [2]

Desktop-publishing capabilities require a computer, printer, scanner, and software programs. Technology continues to improve. After careful research, an organization should select the system that meets it's desktop-publishing needs and stays within budget constraints. For nonprofits that already have desktop publishing capabilities, it is worthwhile to periodically review these capabilities to determine if a system needs to be updated to maximize efficiency.

What are pertinent factors to consider? One is speed. How quickly will the system run? With today's technology, this is no longer the major issue it once was. However, speed may be a reason to upgrade the public relations department's computer.

Disk space is another critical factor. What is the storage capacity of the hard drive? Bigger is better when designing a newsletter. This is because photos, illustrations, and other art require hard-drive space. Memory capability, also known as random access memory or RAM, must be carefully considered, too. Sophisticated design and word-processing packages demand memory. Depending upon the age of the system, the department may not be able to use new software because of the system's disk space and/or available RAM. If the public relations department has a computer, check the hard disk space and the RAM before investing in software.

It is best to check with local printers regarding compatible software and the ability to forward a diskette or modem material. By taking this precaution prior to purchasing a system, the nonprofit can identify the most user-friendly option for in-house personnel and the most cost-effective with a printer.

A HISTORICAL PERSPECTIVE ON NEWSLETTERS

Before discussing today's newsletters, it is beneficial to review the origin of this medium. Newsletters began in the sixteenth century. The first known example of a newsletter is attributed to Count Philip Edward Fugger (1546-1618) of Augsburg, Germany. Fugger distributed loose, handwritten sheets reporting business news that originated from trade centers in Europe and overseas ports. This publication was issued only to paying subscribers. In Amsterdam, in 1620, three printers issued "corantos." This commercial and political news publication was translated into English onto a single page and sold in London. In 1704 in America, the *Boston News-Letter* made its debut.

More newspapers and magazines appeared in the 1800s. When this happened, newsletter popularity declined. However, by 1900, this medium began to reclaim its former position. One reason was because the business and financial communities wanted more specialized news than what was offered by the popular press. One example was *Babson's Reports*, founded in 1904 by Roger W. Babson of Wellesely, Massachusetts. An investment advisory, this publication even carried analyses and forecasts. The first modern newsletter, the *Whatley-Eaton Report*, debuted in 1918. Then, in 1923, *Kiplinger Washington Newsletter* appeared. Willard Kiplinger's well-known newsletter and format have been widely imitated ever since. [3] Interestingly, all three publications developed content by targeting specific markets.

Today, newsletters continue to gain popularity. Why? Few people read a newspaper or magazine from cover to cover. Newsletters provide capsulized information and are portable. Also, people demand specific information about special interests. This need, first expressed in the early 1900s, is more relevant than ever, as the concept of narrowcasting plays an increasingly strategic role in today's marketing and public relations plans.

In the early 1970s, Ray E. Hiebert, then dean of the School of Journalism at the University of Maryland, forecasted that the age of mass communication was ending with the emerging focus on personal communications. This opinion suggests a departure from the mass media movement toward a more personalized and less formal format. Of course, such a style is integral to newsletters.

Editors become known as specialists in their narrowly defined fields of discussion. Consequently, these editors are likely to take a stand or make a prediction, displaying authority. A newsletter also seems to offer "inside information," which is enjoyed by many readers and seems to generate a personal touch not generally found in the mass media. [4]

Timeliness is another attribute. Because it is a simple publication, newsletter preparation time is short. This permits "breaking issues" to be researched, discussed, and distributed quickly, something a monthly niche market magazine is unable to do.

WHY A NEWSLETTER?

Everyone understands what a newsletter is, but why publish one? What is the motivation for putting the PR department through the rigors of producing this publication? If the answer is "because everyone else does," or "the executive director said so," or "our president thought it would be nice," the nonprofit is making this decision for the wrong reason. A newsletter is a communications tool that can help strategically execute the public relations and marketing plans.

By utilizing news articles, feature stories, lists, photographs, and a wide variety of graphic devices, the following goals can be achieved:

• Communicate newsworthy information about the nonprofit.
• Introduce potential donors to the nonprofit.

- Motivate existing donors to continue to contribute to the organization.
- Market services provided by the agency.
- Recognize various contributions made by volunteers, such as financial, time, length of service, training completed, special donations, etc.
- Recognize staff for work well done, length of service, training, etc.
- Educate those already familiar with the organization, increasing their awareness level.
- Demonstrate the nonprofit is a good steward of funds.
- Improve morale.
- Increase membership base.
- Justify the nonprofit's existence by describing the organization's contributions to the community.
- Appeal to the "human side" of readers, sharing emotional stories or personal experiences.
- Entertain readers.
- Update the audience on state, local, or federal government regulations impacting the agency.
- Share success stories of the agency and of its volunteers and staff.
- Remind readers of the purpose of the nonprofit and keep the mission statement visible.

Can a single newsletter achieve this lengthy list of objectives? The answer is "no," or a more appropriate response may be "not effectively." To make strategic use of this publication, specific objectives must be stipulated. For example, is the primary purpose of the newsletter to be recognition? Or is it to explain the mission of the nonprofit, and how the entity reached such a goal? Perhaps the thrust of the publication is to inform readers about legislative matters that impact—possibly even threaten—the existence of the nonprofit. Whatever is identified as the primary purpose of the newsletter, this decision must serve as the guiding principle to determine what topics are addressed and what changes, if any, occur in the publication's content.

Publication goals and subject matter now must be considered in relationship to the audience. Three components identify the reader: demographics, psychographics, and geographics. [5]

Demographics refer to data such as age, gender, education, income, and profession. These characteristics are easily quantifiable and imply generalities about the target group. Not only will this insight help to formulate the newsletter's goals, it will contribute to decisions regarding writing style and design.

Psychographics provide insight into the attitude and behavior of the audience. It probes the "why" and the "motivation," not simply what the audience stands for or believes. Such knowledge is extremely helpful in planning the editorial calendar, selecting the most appropriate angle from which to discuss certain topics, and identifying the motivators.

Geographic information identifies where potential readers are located or reside. For the nonprofit that is simply distributing the newsletter in-house, such detail may not be crucial. However, if the nonprofit has a national or international mailing list, creating and updating the distribution register are challenging tasks.

These three defining characteristics categorize a newsletter's readership, but more research is required to clearly understand who the audience is. First, what is the level of awareness, and how does this translate into activity? Communications researcher James Grunig classified target publics into three categories: *latent* public, *aware* public, and *active* public. The latent group includes those impacted by an issue or an event but who are not yet aware of the impending situation. The aware public recognizes that an issue exists and that it impacts them. The active public organizes to affect what is impacting them. [6]

Once a reader profile is developed, what does it mean to the newsletter staff? The active public has already formed an opinion on issues and situations. They may look to the newsletter editor to offer suggestions about what they can do to make a difference. If a newsletter offers a point of view contrary to that of the active public, extensive detail and numerous facts are required to convince this target audience to change sides. Meanwhile, the aware audience seeks information to assist them in forming an opinion. The latent public must be informed and persuaded to support the editor's point of view.

One way to gather this information is to develop a reader profile. Audience information can be collected in a number of ways. A formal survey can be conducted by an outside firm. Secondary research from the library, databases, or even the local chambers of commerce may provide pertinent details. For example, government documents, such as *American Statistics Index* (ASI), or Simmons Market Research Bureau's *Study of Media and Markets* have demographic details. The nonprofit may already have data that reveals information about its audience and only has to categorize the data.

Thomas Bivens, in *Fundamentals of Successful Newsletters*, poses seven questions pertinent to the development of a readership profile:

1. Who are your readers, including appropriate demographic information?
2. Where are your readers, including pertinent geographic data?
3. What do your readers already know about the topics or issues you plan to cover in your newsletter?
4. What media do your readers already use to obtain information about the issues or topics you will cover?
5. If you are attempting to persuade or advocate a particular point of view, how do your readers currently feel about your subject?
6. What is your audience's attitude toward you (or your organization)?
7. How do you hope to influence your target audience through your newsletter? [7]

Other questions to ask include:

- What do your readers need to know?
- What do your readers want to know?
- What motivates your readers?
- How can your readers benefit from the newsletter? [8]

Does this mean limitations are in place regarding what can be accomplished by a single newsletter? The answer is "yes." In fact, depending upon the size and scope of the nonprofit, the public relations department may publish more than one newsletter. For example, a large hospital could have one newsletter for staff, another for the community, and yet another for special interest groups such as seniors.

A technique used to bring focus to newsletter plans and clarity to objectives is to develop a simple mission statement based on the nonprofit's objectives and audience research. Concisely worded, this statement recognizes the publication's general content and intended audience in fewer than twenty-five words. This definitive declaration is critical to the ultimate success of the newsletter, because it acts as a premise on which editorial and design decisions are based.

ORGANIZING THE PROCESS

Once armed with a mission statement, other factors can now be addressed. One of the first considerations is budget. Budget is a driving force in the newsletter production process, as it impacts frequency, design, copy, and printing. For example, a limited budget may preclude any use of pictures and limit the publication to one color of ink. An extensive budget may support use of color and photos. Based on budget and the required quantity, it can be determined if the document should be printed, photocopied, or color copied. Even the distribution process is impacted by budget, as a cost is associated with bulk mailing.

If the budget is not mandated, the public relations department needs to compute the anticipated cost to create the newsletter. The following list of considerations must be factored into the budget:

1. Will the writing be handled by the PR department in-house or will this work be contracted?
2. Will the design work be handled internally or a designer hired?
3. Will computer hardware and/or software be upgraded or purchased?
4. Will photographs be used? If so, will a professional be hired, or will members of the department take the pictures?
5. What supplies must be purchased initially or ongoing costs incurred, such as film, a camera, photo processing, etc.?
6. How many colors will be used to print the publication, or will full-color process be used?
7. What quantity is required?
8. How long will the publication be?
9. How frequently will it be issued?

10. Will the publication be printed or taken to a quick copy shop?
11. How will the newsletter be distributed (bulk mailing, first-class postage, interoffice mailing)?

All of these issues have associated costs. In order to develop an accurate budget, each question must be answered. In some cases, subsequent questions materialize and require a response before a budget prediction is possible.

The next step is to develop an editorial calendar. This calendar plans the newsletter's topics for the year. By mapping out subject matter in advance, a structure is created to permit newsletter communications objectives to be achieved while accommodating new ideas within a basic context.

It also enables the editor to have appropriate personnel, such as the nonprofit's executive director, review and conceptually approve the planned material. Such an approach ensures the editorial plan adheres to the department's communications objectives and, more important, reassures management that the publication plays an integral role in the nonprofit's public relations and marketing efforts.

With the editorial calendar completed, a work schedule is developed. It is best to start at the distribution date and work backward during this process. The size of the publication, the staff, outside resources, and the frequency with which the newsletter is produced dictate the amount of time allotted for each component:

- Issue planning.
- Research and interviews for content and articles.
- Drafting of articles.
- Approval by executive director, interviewees, or other appropriate personnel.
- Rewrites and subsequent approval process.
- Editing of work submitted by guest columnists, in-house reporters, etc.
- Photography assignments.
- Photography review and selection.
- Art created, if any.
- Design work (thumbnail sketch, a rough layout).
- Approval of rough layout.
- Final layout.

- Proofreading of laser copy.
- Review and approval of blueline.
- Printing or quick copy.
- Ordering mailing labels.
- Distribution.
- Thank-you notes to contributors.

The time frame allocated for each step is compiled into an annual master calendar in which dates and deadlines are specified. This methodical approach keeps the process on target and permits timely publication distribution, an important aspect of this particular print media.

NEWSLETTER VOCABULARY

Before embarking on the next step, the basic components should be examined. All newsletters have the following elements, despite a range in design creativity.

The newsletter title is displayed as a *nameplate.* Typically, the nameplate is set in large, distinctive type and appears in the top portion on the front cover. However, there are variations where it runs vertically along the left side of the front cover or is positioned in the middle of the publication.

Because the nameplate is such a strong identifying feature, it does not change from issue to issue. In fact, it typically remains standardized from year to year. It is also preferable to create a unique nameplate that accurately reflects the organization's image. Consequently, great care is required when selecting the design.

The *folio* frequently appears with the nameplate. It contains the date and the volume and issue numbers.

The *masthead* cites the address and telephone of the organization as well as the names and positions of those associated with the newsletter. Subscription rates and information appear in this section. Most of the time, the masthead appears on the second page of the newsletter.

Most newsletters have *headers* and *footers*. The space at the top of each page is called the header and at the bottom of each page is referred to as the footer. Information found in these locations includes the title of the publication, date or issue, and page numbers.

Body copy serves as the foundation of the newsletter. These are the articles that appear in column format throughout the publication.

Bylines cite the authors of articles. Bylines appear at the beginning of the article beneath the headline or at the end of the story.

Captions identify photographs or artwork. Any time a picture or graphic is used in a newsletter, readers want to know what the visual is or why it is used. A caption, also known as a cutline, accompanies each visual to clarify its meaning and purpose for readers.

End signs are the symbols that signify the end of an article. The sign can be any extended character from a typeface. A journalistic style, such as three number signs grouped together (###) or the number "30" (-30-), can also be adopted.

Headlines notify the reader about the subject matter in the article that follows. Cleverly written headlines grab reader attention, pulling the audience into the article. A headline is brief and written in large and/or distinctive type, so it stands out from the body copy.

Mug shots may appear at the post office, but they frequently appear in a newsletter as well. Mug shots are small, close-ups of individuals, often used for recognition purposes.

If an article is continued on a different page or is a continuation of an article from a previous page, *jumplines* assist readers in following the story. These cues are brief, such as "continued from page 1" or "continued on page 5."

Pull quotes are short phrases taken from an article that express key points or are particularly noteworthy. These phrases are copied from the text verbatim and printed in a distinctive typeface to draw attention. Pull quotes also add graphic appeal to the layout of the article.

A *sidebar* is a brief article that supplements a longer story by adding detail or perspective to the subject matter. The sidebar is positioned next to the larger article.

Subheads are used to break up long stories. These mini-headlines serve two purposes. First, large blocks of text become more manageable for readers when they are broken into components by these visual breaks. Plus, for those deciding if they want to read an article or not, subheads can be skimmed, providing an overview of the article for the prospective reader.

Although not required, a *table of contents* often appears on the front cover, because of its ability to catch reader attention and draw the audience inside.

Incorporating a *mailing area* into the newsletter design is imperative, if the document is a self-mailer. Many times, this section appears on the back page. Sufficient space for the return address and the mailing label is required. Because of the cost advantage of bulk mailing, a preprinted postmark is included on newsletters with a large distribution list.

DESIGN FEATURES

Most newsletters adhere to the traditional 8 ½″ × 11″ format and range from one to twenty-four or more pages in length. However, newsletters vary significantly in size and length. [9] When creating a newsletter or determining if an existing newsletter needs a facelift, one of the first decisions that must be made is which *grid* will work best? A "grid" is a matrix of horizontal and vertical lines that guides the layout process by establishing a pattern to place text and art. Use of a grid expedites the layout process, because there is an established format to follow. (See Figure 3.1.) A grid with one, two, three, four, or five columns can be used. Although many newsletters rely on the one-, two-, and three-column formats, it's been predicted these formats will become passé in favor of the flexibility that five- and even seven-column styles offer. [10]

Selecting a Grid

A well-designed grid, or template, leaves sufficient white space at the top, bottom, and sides of a page to add flexibility to the layout so as not to overwhelm the reader with copy. Page margins separate columns of type and visuals from each other as well as from the edges of the page. An important design element, page margins establish a horizontal or vertical orientation. Narrow margins with wide, text-filled columns have a horizontal appearance; whereas, narrow columns of type with wide margins appear vertically oriented. [11]

A word of caution: Although desktop publishing makes a multiple column layout easier to produce, a novice newsletter designer

FIGURE 3.1

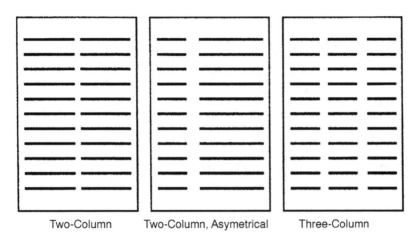

Two-Column   Two-Column, Asymetrical   Three-Column

must understand basic design principles before attempting a complex layout, such as with five or seven columns. Otherwise, there is a great likelihood that a cluttered look will result. The advantages and disadvantages of each template must be analyzed before determining which is the most appropriate. An overview of the various types follows:

Single-Column Grid

The single-column format is easy to design. This newsletter style is quickly formatted, because copy stretches across the page. Consequently, this grid is very convenient for a daily or even a weekly publication. The wide column creates the look of a personal letter announcing late-breaking news. [12] But with this style, the long lines tend to reduce readability. According to a study conducted by Colin Wheildon, 38 percent of those surveyed found body type with more than sixty characters per line to be very difficult to read. In fact, 22 percent of those same respondents indicated they were not likely to read widely set body copy. [13] Large margins reduce this problem but do not eliminate it. [14]

Two-Column Grid

Readers are accustomed to reading a two-column format in text-books and other formal communications. Consequently, this pattern projects a "classic" look. Since it is advisable to make lines of text in body copy shorter than five inches, [15] two equal columns create a comfortable line length for reading. This format is particularly effective when using larger type.

A two-column layout is easy to prepare even with a word-processing program. [16] However, this template is limited in its design possibilities. In fact, it is difficult to achieve visual balance when highly creative techniques are employed. [17] Because of the lack of design options, this format may become visually boring.

Three-Column Grid

The three-column format is one of the most common newsletter formulas. This grid provides greater flexibility than the single- or two-column format. The shorter line length also keeps the average number of words per line at an easy-to-read level. [18] With three columns, it is easier to add visual cues for the reader, and it allows for greater typographic flexibility. Charts and photographs can be woven into the layout with greater ease. Headline length can be varied as well. Sidebars can be added to break up a possibly monotonous symmetry. [19]

Four-Column Grid

Although the four-column format offers design flexibility, special attention must be paid to typography. Narrow columns necessitate the use of relatively small type. This format works well for single-page or two-sided newsletters where articles tend to be short, approximately four or five paragraphs in length. Of course, the ability to incorporate photos, sidebars, and illustrations keep the publication reader-friendly, even with smaller type. [20]

Five-Column Grid

The five-column format is tremendously flexible, because it accommodates long and short articles. This design is based on two double-columns of type with a single narrow empty column. The narrow column of white space typically appears on the left side of the left page and the right side of the right-hand page, thus creating a frame. Headlines can begin in the white space adjacent to the columns to which they pertain, signaling a new article. Subheads can be placed in the adjacent white space as well, rather than incorporated into the text. Other newsletter features, such as the table of contents or pull quotes, work extremely well in this area. [21]

The Nameplate

The public relations professional must always be cognizant of the image projected by the organization. If the newsletter's nameplate does not send a positive image, then it is time for a facelift. If the PR pro is creating a newsletter for the nonprofit, certain attributes must be incorporated into the design process. This checklist is helpful in updating an existing newsletter banner or creating one:

1. The typeface and design should reflect the identity of the nonprofit.
2. The typeface should reflect the newsletter's message and editorial focus.
3. Emphasize the most important word (s) in the name of the newsletter when designing the nameplate. Unnecessary words should be eliminated. Supporting words should be reduced in size.
4. Be sure the nameplate is properly positioned in relationship to the grid format.
5. Check into use of screened or reversed backgrounds, two-color design, bleeds, and other graphic devices to emphasize the publication's name.
6. Repeat the newsletter name inside the publication, but reduce type size to accommodate the inside format. [22]

Layout Features

In the annual report chapter, a few design features were addressed. Therefore, these same topics are not fully discussed again.

However, additional remarks on some of these elements and how these components relate to newsletter design are addressed in this section.

Type

Type selection is based on a wide variety of factors and reviewed in conjunction with the role that the type plays in the layout. Although a typeface may not change the meaning of the words, its appearance enhances or detracts from the message it communicates. So, what image is the typeface projecting through its nameplate, or what attitude or feeling should the type communicate when one looks at body copy or headlines? A publication can project the following moods or personalities simply by altering its typeface:

Trendy—This represents fads or the "current look." Avant Garde type tends to project a leading-edge appearance associated with being current. Its characters are refreshing and modern.

Nostalgic—Bodoni is a nostalgic-looking type because it has earned respect over the years and remains popular, even though it has the "feel" of the late nineteenth and early twentieth centuries.

Classic—A quiet, natural, classic look is portrayed by thick and thin strokes that represent elegance. Goudy and Caslon are typefaces that possess these qualities.

Friendly—Optima is considered friendly, conveying feelings of warmth and personal communication. This is achieved by the easy-to-read, comfortable appearance found in this type.

Informative—When you want to mean business, Times Roman or New Century Schoolbook get to the point. Highly legible and not decorative, these typefaces have a straightforward appeal. [23]

When selecting type, the following components must be examined:

Size—In a newsletter, a smaller point size is appropriate for the captions and body text whereas a larger type is appropriate for headlines. The most common point size for newsletter body copy is 10 or 11 point. [24]

Typeface—A serif typeface for the text contrasted with a sans serif type for headlines works well together. [25] Most desktop-publishing systems have common typefaces, such as Times Roman, Optima, and Helvetica. These types are easy to read. [26] A condensed typeface can display headlines effectively, packing more words into a smaller space. It is also considered an up-to-date style. [27] Text typeface should vary from that used in the headline.

Examples:

This sentence is written in 12-point Garamond type, a serif type.

This sentence is written in 12-point Times Roman, also a serif type.

This 11-point Arial is an example of a sans serif type.

Notice how close together these letters are when written in a 12-point Gill Sans Condensed.

Weight—The size and contrast created by using different stroke weights makes a difference in the design's appearance.

Style—Will boldface or italics be added for variety? Some newsletters write cutlines in two different styles: a bold type used similarly to a headline followed by regular type that contains additional explanation.

Case—Will uppercase (UC) be used for headlines, or will a combination of upper and lowercase letters be appropriate? The upper- and lowercase combination greatly optimizes readability. Therefore, the body text should always use this combination. When headlines are short, they can be effective when written entirely in capital letters. However, long headlines should not appear in an all-cap format.

Alignment—Will the type be justified or have ragged right margins? Justified columns create unusual spacing. In some cases, gaps occur between words or even letters that are very distracting for the reader. Therefore, it is not unusual to hear public relations pros prefer ragged right alignment over a justified style. Contrary to this philosophy, however, a survey conducted by Colin Wheildon concluded that the comprehension of readers was good (67 percent) when type was justified. A ragged right setting rated at 38 percent comprehension, and ragged left setting rated "good" only 10 percent of the time. [28] These contrasting philosophies demonstrate the ongoing battle over justified or unjustified type.

Leading—The space between the lines of type is referred to as "leading." When creating the newsletter and using a word-processing program, the automatic setting possibly should be adjusted to better accommodate the layout, particularly for headlines. In most cases, it is standard to lead 2 points, so 12-point type is leaded at 14 points. This means that the space between the lines is the same as the point size of the type being used plus 2 points. It is not uncommon to reduce the leading by 1 point to save space. The effect on readability is usually negligible if this is done. [29]

Kerning—The space between letters can be adjusted as well. The software package will have automatic settings, but additional kerning is usually necessary for headlines. A professional designer should adjust the kerning as the newsletter is laid out.

Graphics

Graphics add a great deal of visual appeal to a newsletter. Photographs, illustrations, clip art, lines or rules, boxes, background screens, charts, tables, and illustrations make a page more interesting to view.

Lines, also known as rules, are the simplest design elements. This graphic device is commonly used to break up type, separate columns of copy, or indicate a beginning or end of a section. A hairline width is advisable when using a line as a separator between columns. This is so the visual does not detract from the copy. Lines 4-point or greater are used at the beginning of articles, as wide lines tend to indicate a starting point. [30]

With the flexibility of desktop-publishing and word-processing programs, page borders are easy to add. The top, bottom, or sides of a newsletter can be emphasized by using vertical or horizontal lines to outline the publication. Even white space can act as a border.

Screens add color to the copy. A screen is a shade of ink color placed behind text or a visual. Rather than printing ink at 100 percent, a screen is created by printing a dot pattern. Light screens work the most successfully with type. It is advisable to use less than a 30-percent screen behind body copy. [31] In fact, a 10-, 15-, or 20-percent screen makes copy easier to read.

Original illustration is drawn by an artist or illustrator. However, clip art offers many choices while keeping the budget low. Numerous books and diskettes are available that offer complete sets of art based on themes. For example, clip art of sports, the work place, holidays, or school can be purchased. Subscription services offer art on a monthly basis. With today's technology, art can be scanned or imported for use on computer. Quality reproduction is usually very good when the illustration is imported directly from a clip art diskette or software program. Note: Whether using clip art or illustration, use of a single style of art produces a cohesive-looking document with a professional appearance.

Photographs

Photographs provide instant communication, adding interest to the layout. The old adage that a picture is worth a thousand words is true if the photograph is properly selected, cropped, and positioned on the page. This is because photographs portray human emotion and condense information that typically requires several sentences to describe. Whether the public relations professional directs the photo shoot or doubles as the nonprofit's photographer, the PR pro must always strive to get the most from each photograph to maximize its newsletter use.

If possible, the "grip and grin" shot should be avoided. This type of picture adds little to the "feel" of the article it illustrates. An "action photo" is a better option. For example, showing a person's surprise when an award is announced is a creative alternative to the executive director shaking the hand of a person receiving the award. A candid shot of other volunteers congratulating the "award winner" after the meeting is another option. Both of these scenarios tell us more about the personality of the award recipient than a staged picture with a stilted pose.

If people are looking at the camera when photographed, they should be smiling. This way, the subjects appear to smile at the reader.

If the photo is of an authority figure, a desk or other furniture should not be placed in front of the individual. Removing barriers from in front of subjects makes them appear more approachable.

The temptation for the novice photographer is to direct people to "do things" with their hands or arms. This can create an unnatural look as these appendages may appear uncomfortable. Facial expression and body language must match to create a comfortable feeling for the reader. To help people to relax, engage in conversation with those being photographed. The result? Body language is more likely to be natural and expressive, allowing the individual personalities to emerge. [32]

If a photo must be posed, it is advisable to observe the subject during an introduction, interview, or conversation. Gestures and mannerisms that appear in these settings can then be used when positioning the subject. By guiding the subject's pose in this manner, it is possible to create a natural look. [33]

What about the talking head? Unfortunately, this close-up shot of someone talking is a mainstay in organizational photography. Slightly better than a mug shot, there is little improvement other than a varied facial expression. If the photographer includes hand gestures in the shot, a more interesting picture emerges. If the layout permits, a sequence of pictures can be used, reflecting changing emotions or showing progress.

An option to spruce up the beleaguered mug shot is to focus on the subject's eyes. Eye direction, placement, and movement relate to the entire face. An intense close-up of the face, focusing on the eyes, changes the mundane shot into an exciting one. [34] A good "stand alone" picture is one for which the photographer can mentally write a caption, while taking the picture. [35]

Selecting an interesting angle is important. Trying to raise a person's stature in a portrait? Shooting upward is effective, as this angle makes the individual appear tougher, smarter, or higher in stature since the audience looks up at the figure. [36]

Shooting down on a subject or situation helps relate the picture's focus to the context. [37] This unexpected angle creates an unusual visual particularly effective for photographing meetings.

At large meetings, photos can be shot from behind the key subject, such as a keynote speaker. [38] Depending upon the type of lens used, a wide angle, illustrating the large audience, could be produced; or a telephoto lens could make it possible to catch individual responses to a speaker. Both scenarios communicate more than the meeting. The reader can "be there" with the participants. However, if the meeting setting is more important than the participants, the focal point must change. Therefore, it is critical to know what is to be communicated before focusing the camera.

What about photos that do not include people? Many angles are available from which an inanimate subject can be approached. It may not be possible to move a piece of machinery or building, but a photographer can move to find an interesting angle. What if the subject moves? The photographer is still in control. For example, positioning a boat in the left-hand quarter of the frame rather than centering the subject can emphasize movement.

If room permits, sequencing photographs adds interest and visually supports the story. This way, the audience reads and sees the progress or changing emotions. To fully capitalize on the feeling produced through sequencing, the designer becomes as important as the photographer in this process. [39]

In some cases, only portions of a photograph can be used. To solve this dilemma, the designer crops the photo. What is cropping? Cropping removes unwanted material or changes the size or direction of a photograph or piece of art. Cropping does not chop away at the visual but purposefully cuts to:

- Adjust the photograph's dimensions to fit the proportions of the layout. [40]
- Compensate for technical error or flaws in the photo or illustration.

- Eliminate unwanted sections.
- Emphasize the primary point of interest. [41]

See Figure 3.2 for examples of photographic conventions to use in newsletters.

Color

Color is crucial to a publication. It attracts attention, adds life, and conveys emotional messages. Why? Because human beings have distinctive reactions to the sight of different colors. In fact, human reactions to colors are even measurable. For example, red is the dominant color of the hunt, so it suggests urgency, speed, and forcefulness. This is why most people discover their nervous systems are notably stimulated when exposed to red.

Other colors connote different meanings. Yellow is considered a color of hope and activity, because it is associated with the sun. Dark blue, the color of the night sky, is considered to be a quiet, passive color. A general slowing of metabolic activity has been demonstrated when individuals are exposed to dark blue. [42] Gray offers a reserved and businesslike feel. Dark green provides a natural, outdoor look, whereas medium green connotes money, and light green appears to be fresh and young. [43] Orange tends to create an uneasy feeling. [44] Therefore, such subconscious cues must be kept in mind when determining newsletter colors.

When selecting ink color, it is important to obtain a copy of the Pantone Matching System (PMS) guide. This ink-color system mixes colors according to a standard formula. Therefore, whether the newsletter is printed in New York or San Francisco, the ink is mixed exactly the same way. The PMS colors are numbered for easy reference.

When reviewing ink and paper colors, the public relations professional must consider the visual appeal created by the design as well as the image projected through color use. For example, an environmental group may consider using a pale yellow, light green, sand-tone, or sky blue paper for their newsletter. Or dark green ink could be used on fibered or recycled paper. Whatever the choice, the color scheme should suggest earthy, friendly tones.

FIGURE 3.2

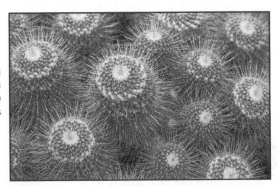

Finding an interesting angle can change an ordinary shot into one that catches a reader's eye.

Shooting upward at an object or person grants additional power and stature to the subject.

Just as white space can be used in newsletter design to set off material, so, too can space be used to emphasize the focal point of a photograph.

Photos printed with permission of Larry Zeigler, Photographer.

FIGURE 3.2 (*continued*)

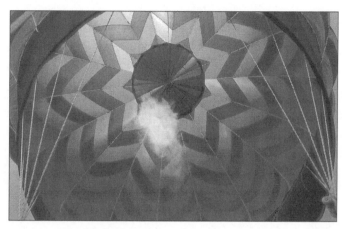

Even inanimate objects gain life when light, fire, water, or similar elements are introduced to a photograph.

An action photo helps to portray the feelings an individual has toward his or her environment. This type of photo permits the reader to see rather that just read about these emotions.

Photos printed with permission of Larry Zeigler, Photographer.

These three pictures use the same basic subject matter but portray a different mood. Be sure the photography properly matches the "personality" of the newsletter.

Photos printed with permission of Larry Zeigler, Photographer.

Color combination can be explored further. The following principles provide guidance:

- Cool colors work well as a background for black type, receding rather than detracting from the type as hot colors tend to do.
- One color should dominate, if two colors are used. The second ink acts as an accent or provides contrast.
- If duotones are used, the second ink color compliments the duotone, unless seeking shock value.
  - Although red can "lift" a page, it should be used sparingly.
- Typically, blue works well as a background color and for reverse-outs.[45]
- It is advisable to print body copy in black or dark ink, such as navy, when printing on colored paper. It offers the best contrast.[46]

What ink and paper combinations typically work well from a readability standpoint? Here are five suggestions:

- Black ink with white paper.
- Black ink with yellow paper. (Bright yellow can be annoying to read.)
- Green ink with white paper.
- Blue ink with white paper.[47]
- Black ink with cream paper.

Paper Stock and Paper Coating

Just as color projects an image so, too, does paper. A thin, plain paper may indicate that the newsletter is disposable. A heavy, textured paper connotes quality.[48] When selecting the paper to best represent the nonprofit, a delicate balance must be achieved. If the paper appears too expensive, readers could view the expenditure as being wasteful of the organization's resources. Yet, if the paper is extremely thin, it makes reading difficult. What paper characteristics must be considered during the selection process? Paper comes in a wide variety of sizes, weights, grades, finishes, and textures.

Size

Most newsletters adhere to an $8\frac{1}{2}'' \times 11''$ format. If the newsletter is run on a copy machine, it is easiest to select from the many papers available in this size. If the newsletter is four pages and folded, an 11 $''$ × 17$''$ sheet can be used. A printer may choose to use a larger sheet of paper, such as 17 $''$ × 22$''$, to produce an eight-page newsletter efficiently. [49] If the publication is to be printed on a large press, it is a good idea to work with a printer or designer to identify the many options available.

Weight

Papers are manufactured in various weights. Paper weight is discussed in pounds. Exactly what does that mean? Weight corresponds to how much a ream, or 500 sheets, of paper weighs. For example, if 500 sheets of 25 $''$ × 38$''$ sheets of printing paper weighs 70 pounds, the stock is referred to as 70-pound paper. Most pamphlets and brochures are printed on 50- to 100-pound text stock. Cover stock is computed in the same manner, but the basic size of these sheets is 20$''$ × 26$''$. Consequently, an 80-pound cover stock is thicker than an 80-pound text. Cover stock is typically 65 or 80 pounds. [50]

Just as paper weight is a consideration in printing an annual report, it is also a factor in selecting newsletter paper. Mailing costs, particularly if the nonprofit has a large distribution list and the publication is issued frequently, can add up quickly. Again, working with a printer or a designer enables the public relations professional to select paper to convey the proper image without being costly.

Paper Qualities

Paper choice influences what typeface and type size are used. An absorbent paper impacts the visual clarity of the piece. Intricate typefaces or small characters should be avoided, so the type does not blur. The opacity of the paper must be checked as well. The visual appeal and readability of the newsletter will be impacted if the ink shows through on the other side of the paper. Should stock be coated or uncoated? Glossy paper reflects the light, making copy difficult to read. Therefore, a larger, simpler type is advisable, if this paper choice is made. Will color photographs be printed? If so, a glossy, coated stock provides a higher reproduction quality than a paper with a matte finish.

The basic paper types are bond, book, cardboard, cover, index, newsprint, offset, and text. Cover, offset, or text are typically used for newsletters. A brief description of the attributes of these three follows:

> *Cover*—Numerous varieties are available, some of which are the same color and texture as book paper but are of a heavier weight; works well as covers for magazines, annual reports, and pamphlets.

> *Offset*—Made for offset lithographic printing; sizing is added to facilitate the paper going through the offset press; relatively inexpensive; available in a variety of colors.

> *Text*—Many colors and finishes available; brochures, booklets, and other work that requires quality printing utilize this type of paper. [51]

Consideration should be given to recycled paper. This paper continues to grow in popularity and sends an earth-friendly message. Since its introduction, the cost of recycled paper has lowered and its quality improved. Recycled paper is available in a variety of grades and varying percentages of pre- and post-consumer waste.

Paper is frequently referred to as being coated or uncoated. These terms refer to the finish on a paper. A "coated" paper means that the paper's surface was treated to improve its printability. The finish on coated stock can range from dull to a high gloss. [52]

Paper, then, greatly influences the appearance, printability, and budget of newsletter production. The "wrong choice" diminishes the end result, impacting graphic elements, the printing process used, and the image the nonprofit hopes to project. The importance of this step should not be overlooked.

Paper grain is worth a brief mention. When a paper machine manufactures paper, the majority of the wood fibers lie in the direction in which the machine is running. Paper folds and tears the easiest when it is parallel with the direction of the grain. Although this is an issue that is of greater concern to the printer than to the desktop designer, it is helpful to be aware of this feature, as heavy paper may require scoring to fold neatly, especially if cross-grained. [53]

Strategic Copy Positioning

An important element in the newsletter design process is strategic copy placement. Readers see the newsletter at three stages: when it is flat or folded in the mail; when the newsletter is unfolded; when the newsletter is opened to the inside pages. Of course, a reader's initial glance is at the mailing address to make sure the publication was properly distributed. Once the newsletter is unfolded, the reader quickly looks at the front or the back page. Since a reader is attracted to the most dominant element on a page, the eyes go first to the photos and illustrations. If there is no dominant design feature on the page and all elements are of equal interest, a reader's eyes moves in a "Z" pattern, across and down the page. [54]

Bearing this in mind, it is important to determine a copy placement strategy. Since approximately 85 percent of all newsletter readers begin on the front page, the most important article should be placed or begin on the front page. In fact, if the front-page story is long, it can be continued inside, persuading the reader to open the newsletter and thumb through the publication to reach the continuation.

What topics are appropriate for a nonprofit's cover story? Possibilities include an upcoming fund-raiser, the kickoff for a capital campaign, reaching a campaign goal, or purchasing real estate. The list is endless, but if the news is considered major or critical to the well-being of the nonprofit, it is apropos for the cover. The astute public relations professional also selects subject matter based on readers' preferences. This information is uncovered during a communication audit.

Does this mean only positive news is worthy of front page consideration? Definitely not. If the nonprofit is facing a major shortfall of funds that jeopardizes its existence, readers need to know. It permits them the opportunity to act. If a legislative battle threatens the objectives of the organization, then those affiliated with the nonprofit should be informed. The front-page feature focuses on positive or negative news, as long as it is important to the nonprofit and to the organization's readers.

What about continuing articles inside the publication? That suggestion should be viewed judiciously. Approximately 83 percent of readers who begin an article do not make the jump to another page. [55] A separate survey indicated that 61 percent of readers found jumps in copy with a continuation on a later page to be annoying.   [56]

With all of this time spent on the front page, does the back page really matter? Approximately 15 percent of a newsletter's readers begin on the back page and work toward the front. Brief news items are effective in this location. Those who turn to the last page first believe that if the articles at the end are newsworthy, copy will improve as one reads toward the front.   [57]

Even for those readers who start on the front page, the back page likely receives a cursory glance when the mailing label is checked. Therefore, an attractive layout and informative briefs gain reader interest.

Even if readers like the outside of a publication, the objective is to get them to open the document. First, if at all possible, photos should be used, particularly action and candid shots. If photography doesn't accompany a story, thought must be given as to what visuals are available and will add interest. Charts, tables, and graphs help clarify complex information buried within the copy. Illustrations provide visual diversion and emphasize key points within the text.

Regardless of whether or not the design accommodates photos, rules and white space can be used to draw attention to specific bodies of text. In this situation, thought is required to decide where a particular story should appear on the page and how this is integrated with the graphic elements to create an effective layout.

Well-written headlines quickly draw a reader into a story. Headlines must be crisp, dynamic, and brief. A long headline fails to "jump out" at the reader and is more likely to blend into the copy. In one survey, 68 percent of the respondents stated they became bored with long headlines. In fact, long headlines generated the feeling that nothing was left to read after finally finishing the headline. [58]

Subheads are an appreciated "reader break" in a long article. This device is particularly helpful to those who skim articles, as these readers look for the highlights. For those who carefully read articles, subheads compartmentalize the data, making it easier to understand and remember.

Establishing a position for regular newsletter columns is helpful to the reader and to the individual laying out the publication. For instance, most nonprofit newsletters carry a message from the president or the executive director. This is not front-page news. However, placement on page two is appropriate. Other routine columns, such as a listing of items or services needed by the nonprofit or a calendar of upcoming events, can be consistently located from issue to issue. This permits reader familiarity with article location.

Design Principles

With a grid system selected, basic style decisions made, and planned content in mind, the individual layout is formatted. The first step in this process is to visualize content position in the newsletter template. Whether the layout is completed in house or if a designer is hired, this step requires brainstorming possible approaches.

Next is the thumbnail sketch. At this stage, a sketch or miniature drawing is created, permitting the designer and the public relations department to examine different combinations of elements and the most effective positioning of art. Once a thumbnail is created, it becomes the blueprint. For the novice designer, the thumbnail sketch is very efficient for quickly viewing different options. Once the thumbnail is completed, computer software leads the beginner through the design process. Of course, a newsletter without photos and utilizing a simple grid is composed easily on the computer screen.

If a more complex design is selected, basic design principles need to be checked before finalizing the layout. These principles address proportion, balance, harmony, contrast, rhythm, and unity.

Balance is best achieved by controlling the size, tone, and position of all elements. Too many nonessential elements in the layout or an uncomplimentary typeface fail to create a harmonizing appearance. Instead, a page appears out of balance.

One feature should unify the layout. White space, borders, or a consistency in shape and size of graphics can serve in this function. However, equal margins can become monotonous rather than serve as a unifying force. So, it is best not to rely solely on this characteristic to achieve unity.

Variety adds contrast to the layout. Occasional use of italics or boldface, not scaling all photos to exactly the same size, and changing the widths of copy blocks by using a multi-grid format add interest to the design. It should be noted, however, that repetition of a few key elements creates the feeling of motion. Long vertical or horizontal elements cause the readers to follow along in the direction the element moves.

Simplicity is the designer's friend, especially the novice. By regulating the variety of typefaces and number of sizes and shapes used as visuals, a pleasing design is created. The novice designer should not try to use everything available in the software. Finally, care should be used with design clichés. Tilting art, overlapping photos, or adding cutouts are effective but become tiresome. [59]

DEVELOPING COPY

Knowing what the newsletter should look like is only part of the equation. The primary variable is the content. After all, a newsletter is not necessary if the nonprofit has nothing to say.

Generating Ideas

Ideas are generated in a variety of ways. The first method is to turn to the goals and objectives of the nonprofit and of the newsletter itself. Questions that must be answered include:

- What is the not-for-profit entity trying to accomplish with the newsletter?
- What information is it trying to communicate?
- What feeling is the agency trying to elicit through this printed piece?

Next, audience interest is examined. What do readers expect? What subject matter is of interest? In the corporate world, data show large gaps among what interests the audience, management, and newsletter editors. [60] The same probably can be said for nonprofit newsletters. According to an employee communications study conducted by Foehrenback and Rosenberg, employees are interested in such topics as future organizational plans, how external events affect the operation, how the institution is competing in the market place, and personnel changes and promotions. [61] It makes sense that those affiliated with a nonprofit want the same type of information. People volunteering time and donating money want to know where a nonprofit is headed and what its focus is. Readers recognize the organization is impacted by the outside environment, including community issues, legislative matters, and fund-raising challenges. Consequently, they want to know how and what the agency is doing in these areas. Who is chairing a committee, who is volunteer of the month, and who was promoted are relevant topics because people want and need to know such facts.

Sometimes readers tell an editor what they want to see. Or correspondence from volunteers, clients, or members of the community offers suggestions. Knowledge collected through this informal means is invaluable, as it identifies subject matter of interest to the audience. Maintaining a file on these topics is helpful when deciding which stories to cover. Later in this chapter, readership audits are discussed. This is another way to obtain input on subject matter.

Periodic feedback and audience evaluation can be solicited through an advisory board. Using this method, a scenario is established in which volunteers, clients, and staff suggest topics and make other recommendations during a roundtable discussion. This open forum encourages an honest appraisal of whether the newsletter is successful and elaborates on thoughts that cannot be accurately described through a readership survey.

When a nonprofit covers a large geographic region, it is difficult for the public relations staff to remain aware of all the nonprofit's newsworthy events. The task of being a "reporter" can be assigned based on individual expertise, geographic location, or interoffice department. Use of these criteria ensures sufficient representation from all areas within the organization.

Monitoring the news media helps identify story ideas. The astute public relations professional monitors current events within the community, state, nation, and world to see the possible impact of emerging issues on the organization. In turn, what is occurring outside the realm of the nonprofit itself and how the individual organization fits into this larger picture is worthy newsletter subject matter.

Generating Research

Once topics are selected, research is the next step. Interviews are one means to collect material. Who can be interviewed? Staff, volunteers, those who rely on the nonprofit, legislators, representatives of the community, subject matter experts, and the media all can be tapped for interviews.

In preparation of the interview, the writer develops a list of questions. This step reduces the chance of the interviewer forgetting to inquire about key information. If the writer's mind goes blank or a lull occurs in the conversation, a list of questions also facilitates the conversation and keeps it focused.

Once the interview starts, paper and pen may not be sufficient for note taking. With today's technology, a laptop may serve as a convenient means to take notes quickly. Also, if the subject matter is complex, the interviewer may want to record the discussion in addition to taking notes. If this decision is made, the interviewee should be asked for permission to be taped.

The library offers a multitude of research options. With the use of periodicals, government documents, books, and even the Internet (access to which is available at most public libraries), many subjects can be researched without ever leaving the building.

If the nonprofit is affiliated with other organizations or is a local chapter of a larger entity, the national or larger association may be an excellent resource. Most national and international organizations have libraries that focus specifically on subject matter relevant to the association.

Writing

The writing style used in the newsletter must reflect the character of the organization. The diction should convey respect for readers. Vocabulary should not be "over the heads" of the reader in the hopes of impressing the audience or "talk down" to the audience. A positive attitude should be reflected. An organization has nothing to gain by conveying a "poor us" attitude or by pointing fingers at other entities; or blaming these groups for loss of funding, a shortfall in operational funds, or a poor turnout at an event. Finally, the writer must decide if the newsletter will be casual and chatty or strive for a formal and sophisticated air.

What are some basic writing principles to follow? First, brevity is important in a newsletter. While being precise, a writer must be concise. Second, clarity should reign. When accuracy and logic prevail, writing is easy to comprehend. Third, verbs written in active rather than passive voice are preferred. Hard-hitting, action-oriented verbs maintain reader interest. Fourth, stereotypes and discriminatory comments should be avoided. This is also true of sexist and biased vocabulary. Such terminology alienates readers. Fifth, eliminate jargon. It is easy to rely on words that are unique or familiar to those closely involved with the nonprofit. However, special vocabularies are confusing to newsletter recipients who are not as closely involved with the organization.

Newsletters rely on many journalistic features. For this reason, the *AP Style Guide* is a valuable reference manual for the newsletter writer. This publication contains common editing marks and is an "encyclopedia" of proper journalistic form. Every newsletter editor should have a copy of this book.

Story Types

What types of stories, columns, and news articles are used in a newsletter? Of course, the answer to this question is dependent upon the length and purpose of the publication. Although basic formats exist, the choices are limited only by the writer's creativity.

The News Story

Newswriting is straightforward. In a newsletter, this format effectively communicates basic information. A good news story answers the questions of who, what, when, where, why, and at times, how. The first sentence in the news article, referred to as the "lead," answers as many of these pertinent aspects as possible.

The writing then follows an inverted pyramid outline. The inverted pyramid arranges the facts in decreasing order of importance.

Such a hard-hitting approach quickly relates all essential information, capturing reader attention. This structure is advantageous when editing, too. If the story must be shortened and the most important facts are at the beginning of the article, cuts are made easily at the end of the news story.

Other characteristics of news stories include short sentences and paragraphs. News stories are relatively short as compared to feature-length stories.

The Feature Story

In a larger newsletter, room allows inclusion of features. A feature story is not necessarily about a current event. In a nonprofit setting, the subject matter for such articles is endless. The history of the nonprofit, a new office, or an institutional tradition are all examples of feature possibilities. Frequently, the writing style is more relaxed and creative than the straightforward news story. This does not mean that facts are missing. Usually, a feature delves more deeply into a topic than a news story.

A feature story lead must creatively pull readers into the article. An *indirect lead* is one technique that can do this. A recap of an event, a brief anecdote, a description of a scene, a quote, and statistics are examples of indirect introductions. The *bullet lead* offers tidbits of information and then ties the pieces together. When discussing trends or stories that uncover the causes behind a situation or event, this format works well. [62] The *delayed lead* weaves facts into the story slowly, placing the initial focus on a detail or idea other than the primary focus. Only talented writers should use this format. Otherwise, it is possible to delay the lead so long that readers are unable to locate it! [63] The *startling assertion lead* offers a dramatic introduction to the topic by beginning the story with an unexpected statement or a surprising theory. The *direct lead*, used in hard news stories, also works effectively as a feature story introduction.

To develop the feature story, chronological and climatic formats work well. A chronological order is used when writing histories, explaining the order of events, or describing a process. The climatic outline is followed when the story builds to a dramatic ending in which pertinent information is finally revealed.

Profiles

Personality profiles add a human element. People enjoy reading about other people. Since many nonprofits focus on people helping people, this type of story is likely to appear in an agency's publication. One of the biggest challenges when drafting this type of story is determining what information is appropriate, interesting, and supports the reason for selecting the subject matter.

In a profile, the featured individual's personality must emerge. When selecting facts and details to describe this individual, the writer must be judicious. One topic emphasizes the relationship this person has with the nonprofit. At times, family history, a list of family members, the person's marital status, or state of health may be relevant. These tidbits go beyond the workplace or the volunteer site and reveal personality, but use caution. It is important for these details to be pertinent to the story line and for the featured person to be comfortable with these references being published. Citing intimate information is in poor taste and invades privacy.

A profile lead alerts readers to the focus or theme of the story. A quotation by the person profiled, a quote by someone who knows the featured subject, or a description of the person's actions can be used to help the reader focus and quickly discover the purpose of the profile.

Interviewing those who know the individual adds depth and dimension to the profile. Trying to look at the world through the eyes of the featured person adds meaningful insight to the article, helping the reader to understand motives and thoughts. Finally, it is best to select a starting point that makes the personality as interesting as possible. Strictly adhering to a chronological outline is easy to write but not very interesting to read.

Regular Columns

Regular columns are an excellent addition to a newsletter because readers enjoy them and editors appreciate the consistency. One routine newsletter column is an article authored by the executive director or the president. Sometimes, the article alternates between the two. The column's purpose is not to patronize or preach. Instead, the nonprofit's values, mission, and goals are communicated and explained. This article also reveals the personality of the nonprofit's leadership. Are the executive director and president passionate about their beliefs and the organization? These feelings are conveyed by the words found in this column.

A question-and-answer format is also a favorite. This popular style is easy to write and read, and it facilitates two-way communication, creating a feeling of "openness." The nonprofit can use this format to update readers on changes, communicate little-known information, and remind the audience of the group's mission or other key data.

An editorial is another example of a routine column. Editorials should be lively and address topics pertinent to the organization and relevant to the readers. Three elements are involved with writing a good editorial:

1. The copy is written in first person. A photo of the author may even accompany the column.
2. An editorial frequently concerns a topic about which the author cares passionately.
3. Editorials are used to share opinions, forecasts, or ideas of the author.

Editorials can be authored by the same person in every issue, or guest editorials can be used. Guest editorials offer flexibility because a volunteer, a person relying on the nonprofit's services, a staff member, or an outside expert can comment on a particular matter.

Other routine columns include announcements, a calendar of events, gossip tidbits, congratulatory statements, or news briefs.

Captions

Photos appear in organizational publications for journalistic as well as artistic purposes. Simply stating the obvious does not add interesting detail for the reader. An effective cutline explains why the picture was taken, who or what is pictured, and other particulars that the reader would not notice or understand without an explanation.[64] The challenge is to accomplish this task in as few words as possible.

Editing

The first rule of editing is to clarify the message and make sure the content is relevant to readers. The next step is to analyze the article to ensure that each thought is logical and that copy flows smoothly and logically throughout the article. Sentence structure, subject-verb agreement, pronouns, and modifiers are checked during the next stage of editing. [65] The elimination of wordy phrases and unnecessary transitional devices protects readers from becoming bogged down in unnecessary verbiage. Crisp, clean, descriptive nouns and adjectives linked by strong verbs keep readers interested.

Newsletter writers prefer active voice rather than passive. Active voice produces concise copy. It is also easy to understand, since the format adheres to a simple formula of subject + verb + object.

Two methods help discover if passive rather than active voice was used. First, passive voice uses a form of the verb "to be," including the past form that adds the word "was." A prepositional phrase found at the end of the sentence also provides a clue that passive voice was probably used. [66]

Passive Example: I was promoted by my supervisor.

Active Example: My supervisor promoted me.

What About the Readability Level?

It is wise to check a newsletter's readability level. Most word-processing packages are equipped with at least one readability formula. The software may use Flesch, Dale-Chall, or Fry formulas, the Gunnig Fog Index, or the Cloze procedure. All of these formulas determine the level of reading difficulty by computing factors such as the average sentence length and the average number of multi-syllabic words.

For example, the Gunnig Fog Index, sometimes referred to as the Fog Index, uses the following formula:

1. One hundred words are selected from the middle section of the writing.
2. In the selected sample, the number of sentences are counted and divided by 100. This produces the average sentence length (ASL).

3. In the same sample, the number of words with three or more syllables are counted. Proper nouns, compound words, and words ending in -ed or -es are not included in the count.
4. The totals from #2 and #3 are added. That number is multiplied by 0.4.

The result of this computation is the approximate number of years of schooling required to read the writing sample. For example, a college graduate should be able to read at a score of 16. [67]

At what reading level should newsletters be targeted? Although some newsletters are designed for those capable of handling a more sophisticated writing style, a guiding principle for newsletter editors is to write for a ninth grader. This is the same reading level targeted by most daily newspapers and used in most general news releases. [68]

THE APPROVAL PROCESS

The newsletter editor or public relations manager determines who needs to review the article or if anyone does. However, it is advisable to incorporate an approval process into the newsletter planning calendar. Why? Distributing a draft for review and approval prior to printing avoids major public relations errors.

A simple form can be created as documentation to prove an article was reviewed and approved. (See Form 3.1.) The approval form acts as a safety net. When officials want to double-check accuracy, this form verifies that those supplying the information had the chance to review and correct the material. A form signed by the executive director proves that management provided input and checked that the publication's communications goals were met. A chair who fails to mention pertinent information during an interview has a chance to add the material prior to publication. A signed approval sheet, kept on file in the public relations department, helps protect the writer and the nonprofit in case someone decides later that he or she did not want a quote to appear.

With holidays, vacations, sickness, or out-of-town travel, two or three days is not sufficient time for review and approval. In fact, it is advisable to distribute a story as soon as it is drafted and to allow

FORM 3.1. Draft Approval Request Form

(NAME OF NONPROFIT)

Date:

To:

CC:

From:

Re: Attached newsletter article draft

Please do not detach this cover from the attached draft. After reviewing the copy, please indicate your response.

The attached draft is

_____ Approved.

_____ Approved with changes, no need to submit another draft.

_____ Approved with changes, submit another draft.

_____ Not approved.

Name:

Title or Position with (Name of Nonprofit):

Signature:

Date:

Please return to the Public Relations Department by: (insert day and date)

If you have any questions or comments, contact me by telephone at (insert telephone number), by fax (insert fax number), or mail (insert address).

Thank you for your prompt attention and assistance.

two weeks for the approval process. If those reviewing the story are unable to return it immediately and if a second or third draft is needed, a significant amount of time may lapse. With proactive planning, even a delay in the approval process does not impact the distribution date.

PROOFING

Careful proofing can save the public relations department from a great deal of embarrassment. However, proofing one's own work is extremely difficult. Here are some tips to preclude errors from being published:

- Take advantage of desktop capabilities. Be sure the document is spell-checked. Although not foolproof, this procedure helps to reduce the number of errors. The grammar checker should be used for the same reason.
- Do not rely on proofreading by looking at the computer screen. Reviewing copy on paper usually uncovers more errors than reading text on the monitor.
- Enlist others to help in the proofing process. Two or three sets of eyes help expose punctuation, typographical, and grammatical errors.
- Try reading the document aloud or backward. Many expert proofreaders use such techniques to locate errors passed over by their silent proofreading skills.
- Examine the copy for a specific error, such as subject-verb agreement or comma usage.
- Carefully check numbers and statistical data. This information is easily spot-checked.
- Repeatedly check the spelling of names. A person's name is special; one of the most likely errors to be called to the attention of an editor is a misspelled name.

Another proofing trick is to double-check areas where readers are most likely to notice an error. Readers tend to notice text near large areas of white space. The beginning and ending of paragraphs and sections within the document also draw extensive reader attention.

Writing experts emphasize that readers pay the most attention to the first and the last sentences, respectively, in a document. Since this is also when the writer makes a first and final impression, it is advisable to proof these statements carefully. Visual elements accompanied by writing, such as graphs, charts, and bulleted lists draw significant reader attention as well. [69] Headlines and subheads also have a high profile. Consequently, a proofreader should concentrate on these specific areas.

So far, comments have focused on proofreading text. Yet, the visual aspect of the publication must also be proofed. Photographs can accidentally be reversed. Are they correct? A clock with backward numbers or a reverse order in a lineup are telltale signs a photo was inadvertently flipped. Cutlines should be checked to ensure correct identification of photos. Are the page numbers in the correct order? Are headlines positioned correctly by stories? Are graphs and tables identified properly and legends accurate? Are stories aligned according to the template and lists properly bulleted or numbered? Because graphics draw the eye, these errors are quickly spotted by the reader.

DISTRIBUTION

Effective newsletter distribution is as important as creating a quality publication. Unless the newsletter is sent cost-effectively and to the correct audience, money and time are spent to produce little, if any, benefit.

Some publications are written for a broad audience. Current supporters, prospective donors, employees, volunteers, legislators, foundations, clients of the nonprofit, and media representatives may receive the newsletter. Is it appropriate to send this publication to all of those receiving it?

If the appropriate people are on the list, is the address information accurate? Continuing to mail a newsletter to someone who passed away five years ago or forwarding the publication to the correct government office but with the name of a legislator who is no longer in office is as much of a faux pas as it is the waste of a good newsletter and postage. Checking with the post office prior to beginning mailing preparations permits the nonprofit to check discounts and mailing options, identifying the most expeditious and cost-effective methods.

To pique reader interest, place a graphic device or teaser near the mailing label. The purpose of the teaser is to lure readers inside the newsletter. Sometimes, logos are placed near the label area, too. It is important, however, not to let any graphic device or copy interfere with the mailing area.

Internal routing may be a possibility. If this is the case, the interorganizational routing structure is checked to determine if newsletter delivery is feasible and efficient. By labeling newsletters and placing them in inner-office mail, employees will be likely to see the publication. However, if the newsletter's content needs to be shared with family members, the publication may never make it home. Thus, this distribution method may not be effective even if it is inexpensive.

Some printers provide mailing service. It may be possible to negotiate a price within the nonprofit's budget that includes newsletter printing and mailing preparation. Because commercial mailing houses are expensive, the nonprofit may turn to others within the nonprofit sector for assistance. The local Goodwill, United Cerebral Palsy, or similar organizations may provide mailing preparation for a fraction of the cost charged by a commercial mailing house. Such a collaboration produces a win-win situation for both nonprofits.

EVALUATION

Designing and writing a newsletter requires significant resources. With all of the time and money spent on producing such a publication, it is crucial for a newsletter's goal to play a strategic role in the nonprofit's public relations and marketing efforts. Of course, the best way to know if PR and marketing objectives are achieved is to survey readers.

A readership survey can be simple or complex. When developing this type of a survey, it is critical to make it easy to answer. Close-ended questions don't provide as much insight as open-ended questions. However, close-ended questions should be included to make a "quick" survey easier for respondents to answer. Length is another critical factor. If included in the newsletter, a brief questionnaire is advisable, possibly limited to one page. In a special mailing to a target group of respondents, a longer, more detailed questionnaire could be used. (See Form 3.2.)

A well-written survey helps the public relations professional uncover several pieces of relevant information:

- What columns or types of articles are read the most frequently?
- What topics do readers want to see more frequently?
- What percentage of the newsletter is read?
- Are articles too long or too short?
- With what frequency should the newsletter be distributed?
- Are mailing addresses accurate?
- Is the newsletter received in a timely fashion?
- Is the design considered friendly, inviting, and interesting?
- Is the design easy to read?

To gain interest, it is also wise to "advertise" the survey prior to releasing it. The survey can be announced in the newsletter as well as promoted during volunteer, committee, and board meetings. As publicity builds, so does interest. [70]

After the reader answers all of these questions, how will the survey be returned to the public relations office? A questionnaire should be designed for easy return mailing. Survey participants are not likely to address their own envelopes and use their own stamps. With the popularity of faxes, a return by fax is another option. Larger organizations may be set up for telephone response. This is certainly a possibility, as people can phone in their answers on a touchtone telephone. Most small nonprofits, however, do not have access to such sophisticated equipment and cannot afford to contract such a service. With the increasing popularity of Web sites, the nonprofit can place the survey on-line.

A tip to increase survey response is to offer something to potential participants. Of course, a nonprofit can't offer a major gift or sum of money to survey respondents. In fact, those affiliated with the nonprofit would probably be concerned about the stewardship of the organization if such an offer was extended. A simple and inexpensive alternative is to enter the names of those returning the survey into a drawing for two free tickets to an upcoming event hosted by the nonprofit. Or, if the organization has a T-shirt or other

FORM 3.2. Sample Readership Survey

(NAME OF NONPROFIT)

Please take a few minutes to respond to the following questions. Your comments are important to us, and we value your input. With your feedback, we can improve our newsletter, making it more interesting and valuable for you.

Please circle the response that most accurately represents your thoughts. We know your time is valuable. So upon return of this form, we will forward to you (to improve response, some small token of appreciation might be stipulated here).

Again, thank you for taking time to share your opinion with us.

Your name: _____

Mailing address: _____

May we call you? If yes, please provide your telephone number. _____

1. Do you enjoy reading the newsletter?
   ____ Yes ____ No

2. How much of the newsletter do you read?
   ____ all of it
   ____ approximately 75%
   ____ about 50%
   ____ about 25%
   ____ at least one article
   ____ portions of articles
   ____ skim the highlights
   ____ don't read at all

3. How much time do you spend reading each issue?
   approximately _____ hours _____ minutes

4. If you don't read our publication, why?
   ____ not interested
   ____ no time
   other _____

5. Where do you usually begin reading the newsletter?
   ____ front cover
   ____ middle of publication
   ____ back page

6. Which columns do you read frequently? Please check all that apply.
   ____ front-page story
   ____ President (Executive Director) column
   ____ calendar of upcoming events
   (List names of all regular columns)

7. Which column do you read the least frequently?
_____ front-page story
_____ President (Executive Director) column
_____ calendar of upcoming events
(List names of all regular columns)

8. How would you rate the visual appeal of the newsletter?
_____ Excellent _____ Good _____ Average _____ Poor

9. Photographs are used in this publication. Do you think there are
_____ too many _____ an appropriate number _____ more needed

10. Do you find the newsletter easy to read?
_____ Yes _____ No
Why or why not? _____

11. When do you read the newsletter?
_____ immediately
_____ the day it is received
_____ within one week
_____ prior to the next issue
_____ it's in my reading file
_____ glance and discard

12. Are there other topics you would like to see covered in the newsletter?
_____ Yes _____ No
If yes, what are they? _____

13. Currently, the newsletter is distributed (quarterly, monthly, weekly). Is this schedule
_____ too infrequent and should distribute more often.
_____ about right.
_____ too frequent. I suggest the newsletter be issued _____.

14. Do you share the newsletter with others?
_____ Yes _____ No
If yes, with whom? _____

15. Do you rely on any of the articles for information to discuss with others in the community?
_____ Yes _____ No

16. Do you save the newsletter?
_____ Yes _____ No

17. Do you want to continue to receive this publication?
_____ Yes _____ No

FORM 3.2 (*continued*)

18. Please identify the age group to which you belong.
____ teenager ____ 20-30 ____ 31-40 ____ 41-50 ____ 51-64 ____ 65 or older

19. What is your association with (name of nonprofit)? (Check all that apply.)
____ personal contributor
____ corporate contributor
____ volunteer
____ paid staff member
____ vendor
____ representative of the media
____ government official/employee
____ client of nonprofit

Again, thank you for your time. Please mail or fax this form at your earliest convenience.

(Provide mailing and fax information.)

memorabilia, perhaps the first twenty-five respondents can receive the item. Obviously, there are a variety of ways to approach this issue. In short, the "gift" is limited only to the creativity of the public relations department and by the appropriateness of the item in relationship to the nonprofit's circumstances.

Of course, other survey techniques are available. If the nonprofit has sufficient resources to hire a research firm or is in the enviable position to have such services donated, market research can be conducted on subjects ranging from if the readers are receiving the newsletter to what motivates the audience to read the publication. Trained interviewers can ask a sampling of questions that center on article recall and probe with greater detail.

Focus groups can be conducted to solicit thoughts on newsletter design and content. In fact, if considering design changes, input from focus groups can be beneficial. This small-group approach permits the public relations representative to show design options to readers and gain input on a firsthand basis.

The option to informally conduct research also exists. Soliciting input from a volunteer over lunch or requesting feedback from the marketing committee are examples of how easy it is to informally conduct research. In such settings, people usually feel very comfortable offering opinions. Plus, these individuals are frequently flattered when asked their point of view.

What happens after input is collected? First, a thank-you note should be generated. Next, people should be notified of the changes, even though they will be noticed. An article should appear in the newsletter, thanking readers for participating in the survey, reporting the results, and explaining the changes.

Collecting input informally over a long period of time? An article explaining a shift in format or content is still likely to be appropriate. However, thank-you notes must be sent to appropriate persons immediately. A thank-you note recognizes an individual for his or her time and demonstrates the value placed on input.

A content analysis survey enables the public relations department to conduct an internal audit. In this communication audit, a representative sampling of past newsletters is pulled. Stories are categorized by headings, including volunteer recognition, fund-raising campaigns, and special events. The results demonstrate what percentage of the publication is dedicated to each category. [71] It is then possible to tell what type of stories dominate the newsletter and to measure this information against the planned objectives for the newsletter as well as with the findings of readership interest surveys.

CLOSING TIPS

Cost-effectiveness is critical for nonprofits. This is especially true in smaller organizations where the newsletter budget is limited. When the public relations staff uses desktop publishing and completes much of the work in house, the following tips may be helpful:

- Avoid bleeds. Pictures and art that bleed off the page may require extra paper and are more expensive to print.
- Use screen tints, especially if limited to one color. This gives the impression that two ink colors were used.
- Do your own photography. With today's sophisticated camera equipment, many excellent photo opportunities can be captured without hiring a commercial photographer.
- Locate inexpensive photo sources.
- If photographs are used, monitor the percentage of enlargement or reduction. It may be possible to "gang shoot" them.

This procedure saves money, because all the photos can be "ganged" or "grouped" together and shot at the same size percentage.

- Do your own writing.
- Double-space stories before beginning the layout process.
- Proofread, proofread, proofread. Carefully proof each step. Then, proof all corrections.
- Use standard typefaces for best readability.
- Preprint color. Use of two-color can be achieved without paying for two-color printing each issue. One color can be preprinted in a large run, using laser-compatible printers. For example, a colorful nameplate and standard design features can be printed in advance. A small number of copies then can be cost-effectively run on a copier.
- Select a grid and adhere to this design, standardizing the appearance of the newsletter.
- Be familiar with newsletter, printing, and photo terminology.
- Know the number of copies that are required by keeping an up-to-date distribution list.
- Take advantage of all possible mailing discounts. [72]
- Always order more newsletters than needed to distribute to new or potential donors.

Chapter 4

The Speakers Bureau

The speakers bureau should be a staple in any nonprofit organization. This is true because of both the ease of implementation of this public relations vehicle as well as its strategic value. In many cases, individuals and groups routinely request speakers from a nonprofit. However, a nonprofit should not assume that calls will automatically materialize or continue on a long-term basis. In addition, this passive approach does not permit the organization to maximize its ability to market itself nor to strategically utilize this particular tactic. Consequently, the effective speakers bureau is an ongoing public relations effort that includes research, strategic market planning, writing, coaching, promotion, monitoring, and evaluation. To develop and successfully execute this public relations task is no small undertaking. In fact, in a small organization, the same individual may be writing speeches, coaching speakers, booking speaking events, and evaluating the success of the project.

Within this chapter, the various aspects of a speakers bureau are discussed and direction is provided for how each of these steps can be developed and executed.

DEFINITION AND PURPOSE

A speakers bureau should be considered a continuous program aimed at:

- Educating the community about the nonprofit.
- Motivating people to donate money or other tangible goods or services.
- Explaining a special endeavor of the group.
- Announcing events or new projects.

- Training and recruiting new volunteers.
- Educating the organization's membership. [1]

This public relations effort is also particularly helpful during a crisis, creating a face-to-face outlet to reach key audiences with the organization's message as well as to dispel misconceptions about the critical situation. Speakers provide more personal contact than a news release that may or may not carry the planned message. The nonprofit representative also can respond to specific audience questions, permitting members of the community to hear the message without media interpretation and clarifying fine points.

SELECTING THE MESSAGE

After recognizing how a speakers bureau is used, the nonprofit must determine what specific messages are appropriate to communicate. It is a good idea to begin by posing these questions:

- What sets your nonprofit apart for others?
- What are you trying to accomplish?
- What is the primary reason for the bureau's existence   (contributions, education, membership)?
- Whom do you wish to reach?
- What is the future of your agency?
- What type of results do you expect? [2]

For example, the nonprofit should have a stock presentation explaining the mission of the organization, its program offering, who benefits from or uses these services, and the types of volunteer opportunities that exist. This approach clearly advises the community of the basics regarding the organization and lets an audience know how they can best support the nonprofit.

Another planned presentation is a speech focusing on the three or four major goals of the organization for the fiscal year. [3] For example, is a new building being planned or a program introduced? Is there a special need for donor support or a major volunteer recruiting effort underway?

Perhaps an annual theme serves as a primary cause around which the whole organization is rallying. This especially may be true if the local entity is tied to a national organization such as the United Way.

This theme-oriented approach should be stressed because the local group benefits from the national advertising or promotion conducted by the parent association. Plus, a theme-based speech frequently offers better audience recall, similar to consumers remembering an advertising campaign or slogan.

The nonprofit may have a set of topics it considers appropriate for any group. For example a health-related organization might develop a speech on cancer, diabetes, weight control, or injury prevention. Such speeches are considered to have broad-based appeal and offer educational information to the audience.

Finally, the nonprofit may have a key message it wants to communicate to a particular demographic group, such as senior citizens or school children. In such a case, special presentations are developed to target this group and utilize an approach applicable to this key audience.

Thus, the speakers bureau develops a variety of presentations to communicate the nonprofit's key messages. Additionally, if the nonprofit sends a speaker on an annual basis to the same community group, or in the likelihood that audience members belong to multiple organizations that rely on the speakers bureau, variety ensures that the nonprofit is not limited by its program offering. Just as television viewers may tire of reruns, the last thing a speaker needs is for an audience to be familiar with the content before the speech is ever delivered.

However, it is also critical that all messages support the basic objectives and themes of the nonprofit. For example, a local chapter of the American Cancer Society may have one speech on breast cancer to deliver to an American Business Women's Association chapter, another speech on teen smoking to present to high schools, and a capital campaign request to give to the local Rotary Club. Although all three have different purposes and address different topics, the objectives and even the theme of each must adhere to those of the organization. In this particular case, the nonprofit's objectives may be (1) to inform the community about the prevention and treatment of cancer, and (2) to create a level of awareness in the community regarding the educational work and support provided by the nonprofit.

Clearly, a speakers bureau needs several presentations. Because creating an effective program is a time-consuming task, topics must be prioritized. Speeches developed first should have the greatest relevance to the organization or be of the most value to achieving the nonprofit's goals.

Clarity of Purpose

Each topic should be examined to determine the best approach for the individual speech. Is the purpose of the speech to persuade, to inform, or to entertain? Although the primary purpose of a speech is established, multiple purposes may result. For example, the primary goal of a speech may be to make the audience aware of a new nonprofit organization, thus informing the audience of its existence. The speech may also encourage an audience to donate to the charity's fund-raising efforts, thereby utilizing persuasion. It is even possible to use humorous anecdotes to make key points, providing entertainment value as well.

THE AUDIENCE

The audience is an integral component in the public speaking process. As the receiver of the message, the audience is the reason for a speakers bureau. Consequently, potential audiences must be identified. One consideration is to determine which publics require firsthand contact.[4] Service clubs, social groups, churches, business associations, educational institutions, cultural organizations, and clubs focusing on special interest are analyzed.

The local chamber of commerce probably has a list of all organizations found within the community. If such a list is unavailable, it is possible to monitor the local newspaper for meeting notices of area groups and to develop a list based on this information. As this directory is reviewed, it is imperative that audiences are prioritized, in order to spend time obtaining speaking engagements with groups viewed as being the most likely to help the nonprofit achieve its objectives.

Once significant audiences are identified, it is necessary to collect information about these groups. Data collected for the speakers bureau has multiple applications. Astute public relations practitioners can utilize this background information to develop a letter requesting funds, draft a newsletter item, or create a brochure.

Scrutinizing Audience Demographics

It is not enough to know what message to communicate. Speakers bureaus managers must also know how to best relate to the intended audience. For example, if the message is reasons why one should quit smoking, the speech writer must focus on the beliefs, attitudes, and values of the intended audience as well as understand the culture demographics of the group. The message can then be properly formatted to ensure communication success: convincing audience members to quit smoking.

In essence, the speech writer must consider "what's in it" for the audience and be able to relate the message in these terms. After all, audience members often discuss an impending speech, hoping the speaker is "good" or "has something of value to say" or "can provide them with new information." In fact, how many times have you thought of skipping a presentation you believed might not be of interest or informative? Although this egocentric perspective seems unacceptable for the mature audience, the writer must remain keenly aware of its existence. For this reason, the speech writer gives serious thought to the interest and value of a nonprofit's planned message to an audience. A speech whose sole message is a request for money and offers nothing in return, quickly minimizes the chance of audience members listening to the plea for funds. Once the writer adopts an audience-centered philosophy, decisions are made regarding the best organizational pattern, most convincing type of supporting material, and best speaker for the audience.

To reach this point, characteristics and likely group traits are identified and categorized to determine the most strategic approach. First, it is helpful to collect demographic information about the target group (s). What can be observed or researched about the age, race, gender, education level, income, occupation, religious, or political views of the audience?

Psychological factors must also be considered. Psychological profiling offers insight into the beliefs, attitudes, and values of the listeners,[5] permitting the writer to tap into what is extremely personal to and develop a relationship with the audience. It is important to define these terms because the nonprofit must be able to relate to these psychological aspects:

> *Beliefs*—Convictions about what is true or false; the way the individual structures reality based on what he or she believes; beliefs can be relatively open to being changed   (variable), or they can be highly resistant to change   (fixed).[6]

> *Attitudes*—What is liked or disliked; an enduring positive or negative inclination; some attitude responses are more dominant than others, such as dogmatic opinion.   [7]

> *Values*—The orientation toward life that provides the standards for judging the worth of thoughts and actions;   [8] a reflection of the principles and qualities considered important;   [9] enduring concepts of what is right and wrong or good and bad.   [10] "Values, then, underlie an individual's particular attitudes and beliefs."   [11]

In fact, understanding the psychological profile of a potential audience benefits the speech writer in three ways:

- It helps frame the ideas within the speech.
- It helps the speech writer select the best/most appropriate supporting material for the listeners.
- It permits the establishment of realistic goals, recognizing that not all audiences respond in the same way to the same material.   [12]

Psychologist Abraham Maslow proposed a hierarchy to demonstrate the various levels of human needs. According to Maslow, the pyramid of needs consists of five steps. The first or most basic component is the *physiological* need. This serves at the human base. Food, water, and air are the elements that support life. Therefore, these needs outweigh those considered to be of higher order.

The next level is that of *safety.* One's need for security, stability, safety, protection from the weather, and freedom from fear or chaos are ruling factors. People must feel safe before they can branch into relationships or be motivated at a higher level of appeal.

The *social* need to be loved and to belong is third on the ladder. The needs for friendship, affection, and a loving relationship serve as strong motivators after basic individual needs are met.

Self-esteem follows. Once an individual reaches this level of motivation, the desire to be esteemed by others; the need to excel or to achieve, to feel prestige or status; and the feeling of self-respect play a role in the individual's thought process.

Self-actualization is at the top of Maslow's Hierarchy of Needs. At this level, one reaches self-fulfillment. With basics and relationships secure, the individual can think beyond the physical and search one's inner self, exploring true potential and maximizing one's abilities. [13]

Maslow's Hierarchy (see Figure 4.1) impacts the speech writing process significantly. It is very difficult to talk to elementary children about literacy if a child's stomach is growling or if a youngster doesn't know where home will be that night. Likewise, a significant financial request made to wealthy business owners who want to leave a legacy is much more likely to succeed than the same appeal made to a parent who is struggling financially to feed the family.

FIGURE 4.1. Maslow's Hierarchy of Needs

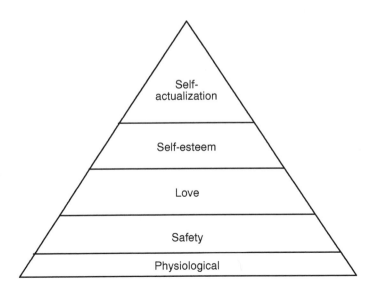

As elementary as this sounds, Maslow's Hierarchy should not be overlooked when developing speeches and matching presentations to potential audiences. One must also remember that motives change and individual responses vary. Timing impacts one's response as well. For that reason, a basic speech must be altered to specifically fit an occasion and audience. For example, requesting support for the American Red Cross immediately following a natural disaster solicits a much different reaction than at a time when a community is not faced with such a crisis.

Fear is one of the most potent motivators. In fact, "research suggests that the fear appeals are so powerful that they actually can interfere with a listener's ability to process information critically. Research indicates that fear appeals retain their effectiveness over extended periods of time." [14] Realizing this, fear can be used to persuade an audience to respond in a particular manner. However, speech writers risk that such a motivator can be misused by or used against a speaker.

Appeals

After recognizing the motivations of the intended audience, the public speaker must examine the appeal or combination of rhetorical appeals to use in a speech. Logos, pathos, and ethos, individually or in combination, should be integrated into the speech design process.

Logos is the name Aristotle used to refer to an appeal to logic. This appeal deals with how people think. Rational people want to examine content and review evidence. They like to believe they make deliberate, logical decisions. The two primary characteristics of logos are evidence and reasoning. When making an appeal based on logos, the speaker cites evidence such as statistics, trends, and facts to support the premise and build a case based on inductive or deductive reasoning. *Deductive reasoning* draws a specific conclusion by referring to general principles or ideas. *Inductive reasoning* draws a general conclusion from specific cases or instances.

Examples of *pathos*, or the emotional appeal, materialize when the speaker evokes emotion in the audience. A touching personal story or a vivid example can evoke feelings of anger, compassion, fear, reverence, or pride in an audience.

Ethos refers to credibility. Speaker credibility occurs through two means: character and competence. Character considers the honesty of the person. Is the speaker trustworthy and sincere? Competence relates to knowledge. Is the speaker intelligent? Does the speaker possess experience or some type of expertise in the topic being discussed? Energy and charisma also enhance speaker credibility. Speakers project energy through enthusiasm for the topic. If a speaker is said to have charisma, the individual is considered to be engaging and likable and may even be thought of as attractive. Together, these factors produce the speaker credibility as perceived by the audience.

THE WRITING

When the writing process begins, the speech topic must be narrowed. A well-formulated thesis or central idea provides definition to the generic subject matter. The central idea is a complete sentence, rather than simply a phrase or a clause, and is written in very specific language. Next, two to four points [15] are identified that support the central idea and are considered of greatest interest or relevancy to the potential audience.

Researching

Once topic parameters are clearly identified, research is conducted. Of course, much information comes from the nonprofit itself. The history of the organization, details on specific programs, and statistics indicating the successful completion of a project are examples of what might be used to support key discussion areas. However, research must not be limited to the confines of the nonprofit entity.

Traditional information resources, such as the local newspaper, can provide insight into problems within the community, supporting how the nonprofit is solving a problem or meeting a special need. Periodicals provide statistics on trends or issues faced nationwide, and a local spin can be placed on such information. Citing material from government documents, surveys, the Internet, manuscripts, and interviews validate the proposition, offer a third-party endorsement, place a trend or local statistic in a broader context, define parameters, or substantiate a speech claim. In short, proper research with adequate oral citation adds to the credibility of a speech and creates strong logical and ethical appeals.

While conducting research, the speech writer must remember that the strength of the evidence has a tremendous bearing on the success of the persuasion. Consequently, research must be tested for its timeliness. Citing old studies or disregarding new revelations discredit a speech, the speaker, and the organization. Validating the reliability and credentials of sources cited within the speech is another important task. Source credibility must be impeccable, if an audience is to accept what a speaker is saying. Also, care is necessary so as not to take information out of context, selectively delete details, or misinterpret an author's or researcher's meaning. Statistics and quotations must be reviewed to ensure precise communication.

Organizing the Content

Once all research is completed and verified, an appropriate organizational pattern is chosen. The organizational pattern plays a critical role in the effectiveness of a speech. Is the oration easy to follow? Does the speech build to a climax or is the key point mentioned right away? Can the audience easily understand the effects of a cause, comprehend how problems can be solved, or visualize a geographic configuration in conjunction with correlating material? Such considerations help the writer determine the basic structure of a speech. This decision ultimately determines the ease with which an audience is able to follow the presentation.

Temporal or Chronological

The temporal or chronological pattern is very effective for informational speeches. [16] The content of the speech is arranged in sequential order based on time. For example, to explain how a nonprofit was created and has progressed since its inception, this organizational pattern is particularly effective.

Topical

The topical outline is probably the most popular pattern for an informative speech. [17] If the subject matter conveniently divides itself into equally important subpoints, the speech writer orders and develops each area of discussion. For example, a speech discussing where a nonprofit receives its support can be divided into the following sections: individual donors, corporate donors, grants, and foundations. Each point then receives the same amount of attention during the explanation.

Spatial

The spatial pattern uses space as the basis upon which it organizes all subsequent thoughts. Arranging items according to direction or location ensures the progression of the speech is easy to follow. [18] The nonprofit operating on a nationwide basis may want to explain which programs or services are offered in key geographic areas. If the choice is made to describe services on a region-by-region basis, then the spatial pattern is employed. Another example is a healthcare representative first describing services offered at a primary facility then explaining services offered by outlying treatment centers. Rather than arbitrarily developing an order for the various locations, a specific order, based on the geographical layout of the system, is followed.

Cause and Effect

The cause and effect pattern is a familiar one. Many times, this approach is used to convince an audience of a causal link between two events or elements. The possible causes producing the effect can be explored first. Or the effect is presented with an explanation of why it was produced. For instance, a health problem could be identified, followed by a list of causes for its occurrence or an explanation about what impact the disease has on the body.

Problem-Solution

The problem-solution pattern is used routinely in persuasive speeches when the speech writer wants to convince the audience that adopting a particular course of action solves a problem. Such is the case if a nonprofit needs to convince donors to fund a new program, because it would solve a social issue within the community. Here, a problem-solution format works effectively.

Motivated Sequence

The motivated sequence, sometimes referred to as Monroe's Motivated Sequence, is a specific pattern for arranging communication to motivate the audience to respond in a positive manner. Developed by Alan H. Monroe in the 1930s, [19] this organizational pattern adheres to a five-step process.

The first step is to gain attention. An attention-grabbing tactic secures the undivided interest of the audience. Although methods for starting a speech are explored more thoroughly later in this chapter, it is important to realize which approach most successfully engrosses the audience. For example, would a rhetorical question draw the audience into the speech? Perhaps a dramatic story should be used. Whatever the choice, it must fully draw the audience into the speech.

Next, the speech writer demonstrates the existence of a need. It is important to convince an audience that something must be accomplished or learned to satisfy this need. This compels listeners to recognize the legitimacy of the claims, become dissatisfied with the status quo, and desire change in the present system.

Third, the satisfaction step presents the answer or solution to the identified need. At this point, the audience is informed about or persuaded to do what will satisfy the need. The proposed solution solves or significantly reduces the problem, so listeners understand and accept the validity of the recommendation. [20]

The visualization step follows. During this period, the audience must be able to visualize a future time when the need is satisfied by following the suggested steps. [21] Any one of three approaches achieves this: positive, negative, or contrast. If a positive method is utilized, the speech describes future conditions if the solution or plan is implemented. The audience is introduced to the advantages and benefits. If the negative method is employed, future conditions are described if the proposed solution is not adopted, thereby focusing on unpleasantness and failure. If contrasted, the speech describes what happens if the suggested course of action is not taken but also what occurs if the solution is adopted. With two futures from which to choose, the audience is persuaded to select the positive course of implementing the solution.

Finally, a call to action is requested. The audience is told what must be done to satisfy the need, what action must be accomplished to transform the desired future into reality. This step must be very simple and extremely clear, because difficult-to-achieve or ambiguous instructions have little, if any, chance of succeeding. [22]

The motivated sequence is an extremely flexible, easy-to-use format for developing an effective speech that can be adapted to a wide variety of audiences. One quickly can see the advantages of employing this strategy in a nonprofit presentation. If the charitable organization is attempting to convince an audience to support a new service or vote on a bond referendum, the speech writer simply establishes a need in the mind of the audience, describes the successful future that would ensue if support is given, and asks for the support. This final step, the ask, is familiar to those working in a nonprofit entity. Although this critical request is second-nature during a fund drive, it is sometimes forgotten on the public speaking platform.

Laws of Primacy and Recency

Two other organizational approaches offering excellent persuasive power and readily employed are the laws of primacy and recency. If an audience is likely to be hostile or skeptical, the speech writer places the most important points first. This limits the chance that the audience will quit listening before the most significant points are made.

By employing the law of recency, the speech writer places the most important information last. This strategic approach is used in the hope that the audience will remember what is last communicated.

Of course, other organizational patterns exist, such as old law/new law and advantages/disadvantages, but these are simply variations of the outlines already mentioned. Whatever outline is selected, it is paramount for the speech writer to rely on the organizational format that will best achieve the purpose for which the speech is written (inform, persuade, or entertain) and communicate the message in the clearest possible manner.

Introductions

An introduction must do more than capture attention. A well-planned intro provides (1) a preview of what is to be discussed and (2) helps establish the credibility of the speaker. An overview prepares the audience for the listening experience. Noting details, such as if the speaker volunteers for the organization or participates in the programs of the nonprofit, further enhances speaker credibility.

Most introductions also include traditional courtesies such as acknowledging the presiding officer of the organization or any dignitaries. A "thank you" to the chairperson for an introduction and possibly to the occasion are also typical introductory remarks. The speakers bureau supplies these customized comments in conjunction with each scheduled presentation. The speech writer may script these remarks or simply provide the basic information. Either way, it is the responsibility of the speaker to appear genuine rather than seem as though delivering a "canned statement."

Drafting a speech introduction is particularly challenging, which is why longtime speech writers frequently employ proven, attention-grabbing tactics. Effective introductions include:

- Startling facts or statistics.
- Quotations.
- Rhetorical questions.
- References to previous speakers.
- References to current events.
- Personal references.
- Using suspense.
- Telling a story.
- Referring to the audience.
- Comments about the occasion or preceding speakers.
- Humor.

All of these examples are likely to be more memorable than a simple, "What I'm going to talk about is...." Yet, the novice speaker is tempted to rely on such a statement. That is why the speech writer must develop a dynamic opening comment.

Caution: Not all speakers are able to use humor. If the speech writer decides to start with a joke or a double entendre, be sure the speaker successfully can communicate the whimsy of the moment. Nothing feels worse to a speaker than reciting a joke and having no one laugh, or having the chuckles directed toward the speaker's failure to elicit the intended result. Also, if relying on humor, derogatory remarks should never be used at any point in the presentation.

Conclusions

The speaker's final words are what the audience is most likely to remember, so the statement must be memorable. The conclusion also provides a summary, which emphasizes the thrust of the presentation. In some cases, a speaker requests from the audience a motivational response, a specific action, or a behavioral change. Whatever the tactic, new material is not introduced at this time.

To achieve concluding objectives, the speech writer may refer back to the introduction, reminding the audience of something communicated initially, providing a sense of closure. A personal reference may be used, evoking the credibility of the speaker and making the audience feel as if special knowledge about the presenter was shared. A challenge may be issued to the audience, especially when a speech is asking for support. At times, the speech writer concludes by describing the future, providing a vision of what could happen, whether it be positive or negative. Or an anecdotal story or quotation may communicate more clearly what the author wants to say. Rhetorical questions are a powerful tool, if well-written, and leave the audience contemplating their mental response. For speech writers who are confident in a speaker's ability to tactfully and entertainingly offer humor, a joke or funny story can leave the audience entertained long after the speech is over. Whatever the choice, only the "finest lines" remain in the audience's memories.

It is also critical to know where and when to stop. Lingering conclusions are fatal. Once the closing is signaled, stop. As a speech writer, you have prepared the audience to applaud. Don't set up your speaker for a long "good-bye" that creates agony for everyone.

Supporting the Speech

Research is cited in the body of the text. This supporting material significantly impacts how well the material is received. Supporting material can be amplified, enhancing the clarity with which the information is communicated. These language devices include: illustrations, statistics, definitions, descriptions, explanations, analogies, and testimonies.

Illustration

When utilizing illustration, the speech writer must determine if it is relevant and representative of the point being made. Three types of illustrations include brief, extended, and hypothetical.

The brief illustration is one or two sentences in length. It drives home a point in a very succinct manner. For this reason, the brief illustration can be more effective than an extended one.

The extended illustration provides significant detail. Although this type of illustration takes longer to recite, it is much more dramatic and emotionally compelling than a condensed version.

Hypothetical illustrations can be short or long. These scenarios are not based on actual occurrences but on what might happen. However, a plausible hypothetical example generally will have greater credibility than one with less believability.

Tips for using an illustration follow:

- Make certain the illustration is directly relevant to and supports the idea or point to which it is assigned.
- Select an illustration that represents a trend.
- Write vivid and specific illustrations.
- Create an audience-centered illustration, permitting the audience to identify with the material.
- Choose an illustration with personal meaning for the speaker, adding to his or her credibility.

Statistics

Statistics are simply numerical data that summarize facts and examples and are considered, by most listeners, to represent "hard" evidence. Statistical information may be much more helpful to the listening audience if it is organized in one of four formats. [23]

Measure of central tendency. The first format is a measure of central tendency, which explains the general pattern of a group of numbers. When a speaker alleges that something is "on average" or that a number represents the "average," this approach is employed. What does "average" mean? When statistics are discussed in this manner, terms such as *mean, median,* and *mode* are assigned.

The *mean* is the arithmetic average of a set of numbers. This number is obtained by adding all of the figures and dividing by the total number of figures within the group. The *median* is the middle score in the group of numbers. If one is discussing the median, half of the numbers in the group are lower than this particular figure, and half are higher. This number gives the listeners a better idea of how numbers are distributed within the group. The *mode* is the most frequently occurring score or number in the number set.

Measure of correlation. This measure explains how two or more things are closely related. However, care must be taken so as not to mislead the audience. A high correlation between two items does not necessarily produce causation. For example, it may be an inappropriate correlation to blame the socioeconomic class of a group of teens for their decision to smoke, solely because the numbers appear to be related.

Measure of differences. This measure describes the extent to which scores differ from the average or from each other. A range is typically cited that is developed by subtracting the lower number from the higher number. A low range illustrates greater similarity, while a high range reflects greater diversity.

An example is an administrator describing test scores of pupils. If the highest score was 99 and the lowest was 43, the range is 56. This number reflects great diversity among the students' testing levels. On the other hand, if the highest score was 93 and lowest was 84, a low range of 9 results, indicating great similarity regarding the students' testing performance.

Percentiles. Percentiles are used to specify percentages that fall below a particular number of possible points. Another way of describing this is to think of each variable within the specific number or score as being equally divided and assigned a value of one within a total possible of 100. Therefore, if 1,000 women are tested for characteristics likely to cause cancer, and an individual woman tested in the 95th percentile, this person demonstrates precancerous characteristics that are greater than 95 percent of those in the test group.

Because statistics are readily believed and accepted by an audience, it is tempting to cite statistics frequently. However, this device can be used incorrectly. The speech writer should adhere to the following principles when incorporating statistics into a presentation:

1. Use statistics sparingly. Statistics should be inserted where they are needed and when they are easy to understand. By simply cluttering a speech with statistics, the speaker becomes a statistician rather than the relater of key information about the nonprofit.

2. Identify the source from where the statistics originated. Since statistics are easy to manipulate, it is necessary to assure listeners this data came from a reliable source. Reputable, authoritative, unbiased sources are a necessity.

3. Explain statistics. Interpret statistics for the audience, and explain the relevance or meaning these numbers have for the listeners. Alert your audience as to the size of the sample, how fairly it represents a trend or population, and the recency of the findings.

4. Make the statistics memorable. Be sure that statistics are memorable as well as meaningful to the group. Round off complicated numbers so they are easier to remember.

5. Use visual aids. Because statistics are overwhelming, script the speech so the speaker can refer to a visual aid. This approach offers the audience two sensory appeals—visual and auditory—by which to remember this complex data.

Definitions

Usually, definitions are used in two ways within the public speaking context. A *definition by classification* is the approach typically found in a dictionary. Words are defined by first placing the term in a generic class or group to which it belongs. The second step is to differentiate how the defined term differs from the other members in this larger family.

Situations may arise when the audience is familiar with the term being used, yet further explanation is necessary to ensure comprehension of the exact usage. In this case, an *operational definition* is suggested. Usually, this definition is original because the term is applied in a specific way that must be clarified.

An abstract term, such as "child abuse," conjures up different interpretations by various audience members. By specifically defining what is meant by such words, less is left to individual interpretation, and the likelihood of the speaker being misunderstood is reduced. Tips for using definitions follow:

1. Select the strategy that is the most appropriate for the subject matter and the situation.
2. Use definitions when they decrease the possibility of misinterpretation.
3. Cite a definition that can be easily understood by the audience.
4. Maintain a synonymous definition throughout the speech.

Descriptions

The purpose of a description is to provide a word picture, permitting the audience to mentally experience, through detailed sensory information, what is described. In a mental picture, the listener sees, hears, smells, touches, or tastes what is being described. To successfully use descriptions, it is important to be as specific and as concrete as possible. This ensures a completely developed picture for the listening audience.

It is important to realize that a description can become too long, creating a mental distraction from the true message of the speech. The speaker then confronts the task of returning the listeners to reality and refocusing their thoughts on the purpose of the speech.

Explanations

Explanations verbally illustrate how something is done or justifies why something exists, in either a past or present form. If the explanation addresses "why," causes or reasons are usually cited.

Employing a "how" explanation, a crime-stopper program may explain precautionary measures to safeguard one's home. The "how-to" list identifies steps that can be implemented easily.

"Why" explanations pertain to topics regarding a policy, a principle, or an event. An example of a "why" explanation is a representative of a citizen's group explaining why one should vote for a bond referendum. Another situation is a speaker from the American Red Cross explaining what circumstances produced a blood shortage.

Analogies

An analogy is simply a comparison. Literal and figurative analogies can be used. The literal analogy is often employed by people who wish to influence public policy. [24] Should city government require its residents to recycle? In this case, the speaker compares two things that are similar, such as the benefits received through recycling efforts in a city of comparable size and the potential of the selected community. The key to this analogy is the similarity. A figurative analogy is less concrete. It relies on imagination and insights rather than on statistics or hard facts.

Testimony

Testimony is the quotation or paraphrase that originates directly from another individual or can be found as quotes in existing documentation. As such, a testimony may be a personal experience, an interpretation of facts or statistics, or a form of opinion.

Testimony falls into three categories: expert, prestige, and peer. *Expert testimony* refers to people who are acknowledged as authorities in their fields. When citing such testimony, it is beneficial to denote qualifications of the individual that lead one to identify the person as an expert. *Prestige testimony* is related to the status or prominence of the person giving testimony. [25] When a celebrity is quoted, a tie-in to the authoritativeness of the source may or may not be made, but a high level of awareness exists. *Peer* or *lay testimony* originates from those who are close to the action or the situation. Firsthand experience acts as the qualifier.

The quotation may originate from an individual. However, at times, a personal interview is simply not possible. Instead, the speech writer turns to material in printed documents. For example, a literary quotation may be useful. Text from books, magazine and journal articles, and newspaper stories are easily accessible, making such print material an excellent resource for locating quotations to substantiate a premise. When using quotations, consider the following guidelines:

1. Collect memorable quotations whenever you hear them. Having a stockpile saves time and provides options when you are looking for quotations that will relate to your speech-writing style and subject matter.
2. Keep the quotation short. Remember that the quote is supporting material. The audience should recall the message of the speech rather than be able to repeat a quote from someone else.
3. Do not overuse quotations. Testimony is simply one type of supporting material, and the speech is shallow if based solely on remarks made by others.
4. Refrain from relying on clichés. Demonstrate creativity by selecting quotes that the audience will not automatically be able to recite from their grammar school days.

Whether directly quoting or paraphrasing, it is critical that proper acknowledgment be given to the source. To do otherwise has a negative impact on the credibility of the speaker, the image of the nonprofit, and the reputation of the speech writer.

Other Stylistic Language Devices

At times, stylistic devices are employed to make support material more understandable and powerful. A brief explanation of select devices follows:

- *Simile.* A comparison between two dissimilar objects; the word "like" or "as" is used when making the comparison.
- *Metaphor.* Two dissimilar objects are equated; because one item can be descriptively exchanged for the other, neither "like" nor "as" are used in the description.
- *Personification.* Assigning human qualities to inanimate objects.
- *Hyperbole.* Extremely exaggerating a situation or an explanation for effect.
- *Antithesis.* Using a parallel format to contrast two ideas.

- *Alliteration.* Repeating the same initial sound at the beginning of several words in a row.

Restatement. Another language strategy that benefits the speech writer much more than it does the composer of written communication is the technique of restatement. Since the audience in a public speaking situation cannot review previously stated information, it is appropriate for the speaker to repeat key phrases or ideas. In fact, by restating particular words, phrases, or ideas, the opportunity exists to clarify and reinforce concepts. It also may be helpful to restate an idea from different perspectives. This increases the likelihood that more audience members will relate to and/or understand the point. However, mindless repetition is boring.

Gender-neutral terms. Gender-specific terms may offend an audience. In today's "politically correct" society, it is advisable to use gender-neutral words. For example, "police officer" or "firefighter" is more appropriate than "policeman" or "fireman," since these workforces employ both men and women.

Remember, by using a gender-specific term   (1) members of one sex may be inaccurately excluded and   (2) social or psychological stereotypes are perpetuated. Some tips for dealing with gender-specific words include:

- Avoid gender-related terms such as "waitress." Replace these words with an appropriate substitute. In this particular case, "server" is more acceptable.
- Rely on the plural form to avoid a gender-specific situation. This tactic avoids the use of a term that might otherwise specify a gender. Plural pronouns, such as "they," help a speech writer avoid stating "he or she."
- Select gender-specific pronouns in specific situations. For example, there are no female priests in the Catholic religion. Therefore, it is appropriate to use the pronoun "he" when referring to a Catholic priest.

Other Writing Considerations

One consideration is the formality of the speech. When we speak naturally, word choice is typically informal and imprecise. In fact, a conversational style may be very appropriate for the audience.

As Lee W. Huebner, PhD, from the department of communications studies and journalism at Medill School of Journalism, Northwestern University, explains:

The simplest difference between writing speeches and writing other texts is that other texts enter the brain through the eye, while a speech goes in through the ear. It is a simple distinction with profound implications. For the process by which the brain absorbs oral communication is very different from that through which it apprehends visual stimuli. So different are the two processes—writing for the ear as opposed to writing for the eye—that they can usefully be described as writing in two different languages. . . . It also follows from what has just been said that the best way to judge a speech text is not to read it over silently but actually to read it aloud, or, better yet, to have someone read it to you while you sit back and put yourself into the mind-set of the eventual audience. [26]

To ensure an informal speaking style appears on the public platform, the speech writer may not write the text verbatim. Instead, a detailed outline might be prepared. This method facilitates a more natural delivery style, because the speaker is forced to use personal vocabulary rather than rely on the written words.

At other times, a more formal style is desired. In this case, the speech writer prepares the script precisely. Even when a formal approach is desired, it is best to remember the previous advice and focus on the auditory appeal.

Vocabulary and speaker style are critical components as well. In a speakers bureau, a number of different people deliver the same speech. However, if a speech is prepared for exclusive use, such as the executive director or fund-raising chair, the speech writer must confer with the particular person. This meeting permits the writer to learn what aspects of the topic are of interest to the speaker, if any interesting stories or personal examples can be incorporated into the speech, and what speaking style or vocabulary is natural for the speaker.

Use of a tape recorder and detailed note taking are helpful during this process. Questions can be posed, details clarified, and ideas amplified. The writer can even use techniques, such as restatement or asking the speaker to justify thought processes, so insight regarding the speaker's philosophy is gained and properly interpreted by the speech writer.

Subsequent interviews permit the speech writer to reconfirm the basics and discuss supporting material. Of course, such an opportunity permits the speech writer to check primary points and receive approval regarding the use of personal stories, vocabulary selection, and style issues. Although there are no specific guidelines for the level of formality and vocabulary that one should use, it is recommended that language and style be *slightly* more formal than the conversational level of the audience. [27]

A major challenge faced by the proficient speech writer is the capacity to demonstrate an empathetic ability, to think and feel as the speaker does about a topic. In a way, the writer is the alter ego of the speaker, communicating more than merely the words of the speaker. [28] The speaker's emotion and tone are communicated via the speech writer's talents as well.

Actually, the speech writer has many masters. The writer feels allegiance for the speakers bureau. The necessary support of the nonprofit's objectives must be included within every presentation. And, the demands of drafting a speech as well as making sure a speaker feels comfortable with the writing style and content must be met.

Attitude and intensity also impact the success of a speech. The denotation of a word can be very different from the connotation the audience assigns. While the denotative meaning is precise and objective, the connotation is variable and subjective. Connotative meanings suggest intensity and emotional power. Today's audience reflects the global community. What is perfectly acceptable in one culture may be degrading or insulting to those of another. Consequently, the speech writer must be extremely sensitive regarding word choice as well as an audience's sophistication level, special interests and concerns, cultural background, and demographic data. This is why reviewing audience research is imperative. Proper grammatical usage is also a necessity.

Length

How long is too long? When the speaker is on the agenda of a weekly or monthly meeting, 20 or 30 minutes is generally allocated for the program. In fact, this is a practical length, because even a friendly audience loses interest after a while. Since the speakers bureau is most likely to receive a request for a weekly or monthly meeting, it is best to prepare presentations within these parameters.

If a speech is requested for a seminar or special event, more time may be available. The opportunity for a longer program is clearly advantageous to the nonprofit. In this case, expanding an existing presentation or developing a new speech is required. The chance to promote the nonprofit's image or message cannot be taken lightly and must be given special attention when such a situation arises.

Format

Speech text must be in a format usable by all bureau participants. For that reason, a complete manuscript as well as outline notes should be available on each presentation. The speaker can then select his or her preferred format. Speakers can mark their copy of the speech, noting verbal cues such as pauses or tempo changes, personal remarks, or reminders about visual aids.

Manuscripts should be typed in double- or even triple-spacing. Typed outlines on note cards are also very helpful. When details are supplied on index cards, it is best to limit the number of points addressed on each card. If quotations or statistics are used, separate cards should be prepared.

Speeches should be retained in file folders to keep them organized and to eliminate the possibility of loss. When given to speakers, speeches should be in a file folder. This ensures pages stay together, reduces the chance that papers are lost, protects the text from getting soiled or crumpled, and presents a professional look when the speaker strides to the podium carrying the stiff-backed folder.

THE Q & A

The writer should anticipate questions. Therefore, it is a good idea to draft a list of questions likely to be asked about the subject matter. It is also advisable to prepare a list of questions asked frequently about the nonprofit. Responses to these likely inquiries should be developed, too. It is best to think of each answer as a tiny speech.

This is accomplished by following the formula used when writing a long speech: prepare an introductory statement, state the main points that answer the question, and offer a concluding remark. Once answers are prepared, they can be shared with the nonprofit's executive director to ensure accuracy and compatibility with organizational goals and primary messages. After making the director's corrections, answers are finalized.

These question-and-answer sheets should be shared with all speakers bureau participants. This way, if general questions about the nonprofit arise, the speaker can communicate the nonprofit's official response in a courteous and succinct manner without feeling the pressure of being unprepared.

Speakers should be reminded to listen carefully to the entire question. It is critical that a speaker respond to the actual question posed rather than assuming he or she knows what is being asked. Repeating the question prior to the response is a good way for the speaker to focus on the specific question. It also permits the audience to hear what was asked. Speakers also should be warned that several questions may be grouped together and posed in a complex manner. In such cases, the speaker may want to request clarification before answering. Then, each aspect of the inquiry can receive an individual response. Finally, it is best to advise speakers that they may not be equipped to respond to all questions. In such instances, speakers should not fabricate information. Rather than becoming flustered, the speaker should offer to provide answers after having time to research the topic. Of course, it is critical that the speaker obtain the name of the person who posed the question and pertinent contact information, so follow-up can occur.

THE SPEAKERS

The speakers bureau must develop a list of potential speakers. Paid staff, volunteers, and clients of the nonprofit should all be viewed as candidates. When editing the list, considerations include the number of speakers needed, which individuals would make the best ambassadors for the group, the interests of the individual speakers, and the public speaking skills possessed by each candidate.

Recruiting Speakers

It would be ideal if staff and volunteers would step forward and offer their services, but this usually doesn't occur. In most cases, a "call" must be issued, and the request may even require heavy promotion. Logical locations to publicize the need for bureau volunteers are in the nonprofit's newsletter, on office bulletin boards, by memo, or in meetings.

If members of the organization give presentations at meetings or demonstrate natural public speaking abilities when delivering a report, it is a good idea to recruit these persons. If a candidate declines, ask for recommendations of others on the membership roster who would perform well on the speaking circuit.

Speaker Credibility

Speaker credibility and image influence how the audience perceives a nonprofit. Those serving in leadership positions are always good choices. Volunteers obviously are affiliated with the nonprofit by choice rather than by pay and have personal experiences they are willing to share, offering the audience an interesting viewpoint while adding credibility and passion.

Individuals who benefit from the nonprofit can be equally credible and of interest to an audience. For example, an articulate high school student, Girl Scout, or Boy Scout can share with audience members what has been learned through a program offered by the nonprofit organization.

One cannot easily overlook the strength of personal credibility. In fact, the higher the level of speaker credibility, the more likely the audience will be to accept the message. Even though speaker credibility may diminish due to specific circumstances or over time, this personal element even impacts other variables within the communication process. [29] Therefore, using credibility as a qualifier in the speaker-selection process is critical. Questions to pose regarding the personal attributes of a credible speaker include:

- How competent is the speaker?
- Is the speaker respected and considered to be of "good" character?

- Is the speaker similar to the audience, so the speaker and audience identify with each other?
- Does the speaker appear friendly and pleasant?
- Does the speaker appear sincere?
- Is the speaker dynamic?
- Does the speaker possess an outgoing personality?

How can an individual speaker's credibility be enhanced? When drafting the speech, the writer scripts copy that positions the speaker in a positive light. Using appropriate supporting material, selecting evidence that is timely, and carefully wording speech content build reputation. However, a speaker must assume responsibility for some aspects, such as:

- Never apologize for a presumed inadequacy of the speech.
- Seek common ground with the listeners.
- Display goodwill and respect for the audience.

The verbal and nonverbal delivery of the speech reinforces the speaking process or detracts from it. For that reason, a speaker's delivery skills cannot be overlooked.

Training Speakers

Before training and support are provided by the bureau, the candidate's presentation skills must be analyzed. Has the person addressed groups before or had professional speech training? Does the person possess an extensive background in the nonprofit? These findings are weighed against the amount of time the organization can invest in training the individual. A small number of speakers with experience and knowledge will quickly produce results for the speakers bureau, whereas it may take extensive training to get other candidates ready for the speaking circuit.

Practice, Practice, Practice

Regardless of a speaker's expertise or if the speaker memorizes, partially reads, reads entirely, or simply uses notes during the delivery, it is imperative to allot practice time. Practice sessions allow the speaker time to feel confident that the message is being communicated clearly and effectively. This also gives the coach an opportunity to learn speaker idiosyncrasies and what might intimidate an individual when on the speaking platform. Speaker anxiety, commonly referred to as stage fright, can inhibit even the seemingly extroverted person. Knowing such information gives the coach a chance to work out any delivery problems.

Anxiety

In Karen Kangas Dwyer's book, *Conquer Your Speechfright* , she lists four types of communication apprehension:

- traitlike
- situational
- audience-based
- context-based [30]

Traitlike apprehension is linked to a personality type. About 20 percent of the population experiences shyness and apprehension on a one-on-one level. [31] Consequently, this must be considered when screening candidates. It is not that such individuals will never be able to take an active role in a speakers bureau, but the amount of time a coach must invest in such an individual may be more than is available.

Situation-based apprehension is an emotional response manifested by the speaker when communicating at a given time. Such an experience can be brief or even transitory. However, the apprehension disappears when the particular situation passes. For example, knowing that a speech is being broadcast live on cable television can make even the most accomplished public speaker feel apprehensive.

Anxiety can be produced when speaking to a specific audience. The astute bureau professional identifies audiences with whom a speaker feels uncomfortable and refrains from using this person as a presenter to the group in question. Such a move creates less anxiety for the bureau member and is more likely to ensure a successful presentation.

Context-based apprehension is a consistently fearful response to a communication context. The most common example of this is the fear of public speaking. A coach who is aware of the degree of apprehension possessed by a potential speaker can better judge the time investment required to develop this candidate into a dynamic member of the speakers bureau.

THE VOICE

The speaking voice has many attributes, including volume, rate, pauses, pitch, articulation, pronunciation, vocal segregates, and vocal characterizers.

Volume

Volume refers to the intensity of the voice. Loudness is an attribute assigned to the perception of relative vocal intensity. [32] Usually, it is a good idea to speak loudly enough for the listeners in the back row to hear. However, it is best to take a cue from audience feedback and adjust the speaking volume accordingly.

While being coached, the ability of a speaker to project his or her voice can be assessed. For example, is the speaker able to "speak from the diaphragm," effectively using the air in the lungs and pushing the air through the larynx or voice box? [33] The goal is to project the voice without strain and before running out of air. After considering an individual's projection ability and comparing this level to room size, the speaking coach may decide to use a microphone.

Rate

Rate refers to the speed with which a speech is delivered. Approximately 160 to 170 words or syllables per minute are spoken in a typical conversation or when reading aloud. [34] Most professional speakers average between 120 and 180 words per minute. [35]

If coaching an individual who reads a manuscript, be sure to emphasize the need to read slowly. A common problem for a nervous speaker is to recite at too rapid of a rate. When this happens, listeners miss part of the message, as they may not have time to comprehend all of the material. On the other end of the spectrum, the speaker who delivers the presentation at a slow tempo gives the audience time for their minds to wander. A third problem is when little or no variation in delivery tempo occurs; a boring performance results.

It is best to establish a comfortable tempo and strive for variety within that rate. One way to vary delivery speed is to insert pauses. Pauses are powerful for three reasons. First, a pause can be used as a transitional device, providing an adequate mental break that permits the audience to prepare for the next key point. Second, a pause placed at the end of an important assertion allows the audience to ponder the full significance of what was just stated. Finally, pauses placed after rhetorical questions enable the audience to mentally respond to what was just asked, adding a type of audience participation.

By varying the speaking speed and inserting strategically placed pauses, a varied delivery tempo results, making the presentation more audibly interesting. It is also a good idea to pause a moment before beginning the presentation as well as to pause before exiting from the speaking platform. The initial pause allows the audience to "settle in" and mentally prepare for the presentation. And by briefly waiting in silence after completing the delivery, the speaker does not appear to be fleeing from the podium.

Pitch

Pitch deals with the "height" of the voice. In other words, how high or how low the vocal sound is. Everyone has a normal speaking range. Vocal variety refers to the amount of pitch variation within that range. Monotone occurs when variety in pitch is absent. If pitch variations become too predictable, the voice becomes equally as boring. Individuals considered to be among the best public speakers are typically those capable of varying vocal inflection.

As a coach, it is necessary to work with a speaker to ensure maximum pitch variety. If the speaker relies on a manuscript for delivery, it may be helpful to mark specific words or phrases that assist the speaker to remember particular inflection patterns.

Articulation

Articulation refers to the ability to correctly form the sound of each word. [36] Three major problems result from poor articulation. The first one is that of omission, when a sound or a syllable is deleted as the word is pronounced. The second error occurs when a word is pronounced by incorrectly substituting one sound for the correct one. A third problem results from adding sounds to a word where they do not belong. [37]

Many times, speakers are not cognizant of their articulation errors. For that reason, it is particularly important for a coach to scrutinize the enunciation of the speaker and alert this individual to problems. Once aware, the speaker can make a conscious effort to correct this verbal pattern.

Pronunciation

Pronunciation is the ability to say each word correctly, including the proper sound and correct accent. One of the most common pronunciation problems is applying the syllable accent incorrectly. The other likely error is assigning a sound where none belongs. [38]

Although a good dictionary is the best friend a speaker can have to correct this situation, the chance exists that the speaker is unaware of the faux pas. Consequently, it is up to the coach to identify the problem, so corrective action is taken.

Vocal Segregates

How many times have intruding phrases and sounds, originating from the speaker, become a distraction for an audience? It is amazing, but even the most educated and conversational person can be plagued by vocal segregates when on the speaking platform. Phrases such as "uh," "um," and intruding tics can permeate a performance, prompting listeners to count the number of interruptions rather than focus on the message. For some speakers, intrusions multiply as the level of personal anxiety rises. Care must be taken to avoid such deadly pitfalls, and it is the coach's duty to assist the speaker in doing so.

Vocal Characterizers

Most vocal characterizers appear during presentation because of speaker anxiety. For example, unintentional, nervous laughter severely damages speaker credibility if it surfaces during delicate or serious points. Heavy, marked inhaling, another vocal characterizer, creates an audio distraction for listeners and becomes pronounced when a microphone is employed.

Other vocal characterizers, such as moaning, do not appear with the same frequency as laughter or pronounced breathing, but prove to be equally distracting when they surface. Again, a coach must help a speaker eliminate the vocal characteristics because the interruptions impact delivery success.

NONVERBAL COMMUNICATIONS

Sometimes a presentation is undermined by what is *not* said as well as by what *is* said. For that reason, the nonverbal communication of a speaker must be analyzed. Attributes of body language considered critical to the success of a powerful public speaking presentation are eye contact, facial expression, gestures, body movement, and posture. Personal appearance also impacts a speaker's credibility and effectiveness.

Eye Contact

Direct eye contact is considered impolite in some cultures, yet many speakers from Western countries establish strong eye contact with their audiences. [39] A visual connection is one of the fastest ways to establish a bond with audiences. In fact, most audiences in the United States prefer to have eye contact established before the speaker even begins the presentation. [40]

Eye contact is used to communicate confidence and commitment. This personal connection demonstrates concern for listeners that, in turn, motivates the audience to listen to the speaker. It is necessary to maintain eye contact with all listeners, not simply a portion of the audience. This means the speaker's visual range must include even those seated on the far right and far left, in the back as well as the front of the room, but without establishing an anticipated pattern. Poor eye contact includes relying on quick scans of the audience, glancing from side-to-side without making contact, and looking at the back of the room, just over the heads of audience members. At the same time, if the visual contact turns into a stare, a speaker can make audience members feel uncomfortable.

A strong visual connection builds speaker credibility. Sincerity and competence are attributes frequently assigned to the speaker who is able to maintain good eye contact with an audience. [41] Likewise, listeners may believe a speaker is dishonest or evasive if unable to look into the eyes of an audience. Although it is tempting for novice speakers to bury their heads in manuscripts, eye contact is crucial. Without it, audience members may feel disregard or believe a lack of respect is displayed.

Good eye contact benefits the speaker by allowing valuable feedback through the observation of body language. Does the audience agree or disagree with the premise? Are the listeners interested in the topic or not? Do they understand what is being said? By being sensitive to such reactions, the professional speaker can add more vocal variety, take a few extra seconds to elaborate on a concept, or make some other minor adjustments to the presentation. Such responsiveness is sure to enhance the effectiveness of the speech.

The best way for a speaker to have more available "eye" time is to be very familiar with the script. Such familiarity is accomplished through practice sessions.

Facial Expressions

Facial expressions convey a wide range of attitudes and emotions. Although humans are capable of producing more than 250,000 different facial expressions, six are expressed the most frequently. These are happiness, anger, surprise, fear, disgust, and sadness. According to cross-cultural studies conducted by psychologist Paul Ekman, these basic expressions are virtually universal in meaning. [42] With audiences becoming more diverse, the commonality of this communication increases in significance.

The astute speaker knows the importance of matching facial expression with words. For instance, grinning during a somber or extremely serious topic leaves the audience puzzled about the exact meaning of the communication. At other times, the smile is an appropriate as well as a welcome sight for the audience. A smile also serves as a physical reaction capable of dispelling speaker tension. [43]

Gestures

By using hand and arm movements as an extension of the body, gestures help illustrate the meaning of a speech. Although used comfortably in conversation, the novice speaker frequently feels awkward using gestures. Hands seem more comfortable if clasped behind the back or stuck in pockets, but resorting to such an action limits the overall effectiveness of the presentation. Hands should always be placed in the "ready" position, next to the sides of the body. Hands then can move freely and naturally. Allowing hand movement to be expressive and spontaneous, yet deliberate, emphasizes key points, assisting the audience to visualize specific aspects of the speech.

"Open" gestures embrace the audience, creating a stronger link with listeners. Crossed arms and tense gestures pulled toward the speaker cut off the feeling of communication and create the appearance of a barrier between the speaker and the audience.

Gestures that manifest the nervous feeling of the speaker, such as fidgeting with a ring or pen, brushing back one's hair, or playing with a sleeve or button, create a distraction for the audience. Flailing one's arms or making overdramatic gestures also detract from the message. Although it is tempting to plan each gesture and use a designated hand or arm movement, a speaker risks appearing stilted or rehearsed, which creates an awkward feeling for the speaker and for the audience.

The speech coach must work closely with the speaker to maximize the effectiveness of this aspect of body language. As difficult and as unnatural as using gestures feels, this movement improves with practice. Knowing how to smoothly integrate gestures with visual aids is critical to a successful delivery.

Body Movement

The audience scrutinizes maneuvering on and off the speaking platform as well as during the speech. This creates a significant need for well-planned, confident, and natural movement. The ability to walk to the podium in a purposeful and self-assured manner is necessary. Once in front of the room, the speaker may opt to use a podium. A podium, however, is not a place to hide. Even when standing behind this physical barrier, the illusion of movement can be created by small forward and backward moves or by minor flexes in the upper body.

If not limited by this physical barrier, the speaking platform expands, and the speaker can easily add more movement to the presentation. Because any type of body movement draws attention, guidelines should be remembered. First, don't move without a reason. Movement should be deliberate and motivated. Is the speaker trying to draw special attention to the point, or is this a nonverbal method to assist the audience in mentally transitioning to the next primary area of discussion? An overabundance of movement at an inappropriate time distracts the audience from the message rather than providing an appropriate mental signal that aids audience understanding. Likewise, appearing strapped to the speaking area, afraid to move one's feet, makes the speaker look uncomfortable. This discomfort is noticed by the audience and, in turn, makes listeners feel equally uncomfortable.

Making the movement too patterned bores an audience. Once a predictable rhythm develops, the movement becomes monotonous. Plus, without spontaneity, the speaker appears uninvolved in the speech or seemingly without a link to the current situation.

The best advice a coach can give is to suggest natural, spontaneous movement. To achieve this, the speaker must gain a comfort level in front of the group. This, again, is developed through practice.

Posture

Posture also conveys a message to the audience. If slumped onto the podium, a speaker appears uninterested in the subject matter. If standing in a slouched position, the speaker undermines his or her credibility by appearing less than confident.

A speaker exhibiting good posture with the head held erect projects an air of self-confidence and self-assurance. A strong stance serves as a base. Ideally, feet are placed shoulder-width apart, measuring approximately 12 to 18 inches. Standing with one foot slightly in front of the other is another strong stance, because the speaker is poised to move. However, striving for good speaking posture does not mean stiffening the body or setting it in a military stance. Instead, a slightly relaxed and more natural pose makes the speaker and audience feel more comfortable.

Finally, remind the speaker that a podium is an aid where note cards or manuscripts are placed. Touching the podium lightly is appropriate but using it as a leaning post is not. To use this piece of furniture as a type of crutch conveys weakness on the part of the speaker.

Appearance

As a speaker walks to the podium, one of the first things noticed by the audience is appearance. It is common knowledge that first impressions are important and that people quickly make judgments based on initial impressions. A number of studies confirm that personal appearance plays an important role in speechmaking. [44] In the United States, clothing acts as an index of how other's regard us.[45] Consequently, speakers must be advised regarding the most appropriate attire.

A tasteful outfit, matched to the speaking occasion, audience, and topic, may be formal or informal. The "dressiness" of the outfit must match the situation. Clothing also should enhance the speaker's personal appearance.

Color, of course, is a primary consideration. People tend to react differently to the various colors through the association process. The speaker may also look better in one color than another. Color consultants frequently make recommendations regarding what colors are "best" for an individual. Although the particular situation and one's individual look must be part of the color-choice process, general selections should adhere to a few axioms.

Typically, navy and gray are "old faithfuls" on the speaking circuit. These colors are not too severe nor do they undermine the credibility of the speaker. Depending upon the geographic region of the country or the profession, other colors may be considered equally acceptable. Red is frequently considered a "power" color. However, red might be avoided for a speaking engagement addressing the nonprofit's poor fiscal management because of subconscious overtones. Because black can connote severity or a somber attitude, it may not be a good color when announcing the addition of a new wing for a hospital's critically ill patients. Browns and tans may be the best personal color choice; however, these shades should be used sparingly or in conjunction with other colors, as earth tones are frequently linked to humility. Also, dressing in the organization's official colors may be an option, as this can subconsciously communicate support and enthusiasm for "the team."

Flamboyant attire or clothing that is too showy draws attention away from the message. The design and cut of a garment should be simple and have uncluttered lines. A poor fit can ruin the appearance of even the nicest outfit. Therefore, a garment's style and fit must compliment the size and shape of the speaker. In fact, ill-fitting clothes prove distracting to the speaker as well as the audience. A speaker may be tempted to fidget with a long sleeve or may appear red-faced and uncomfortable if wearing a shirt with a tight neck. A plunging neckline on a blouse can draw attention away from the face and eyes.

The basic suit is "man's best friend" when heading toward the podium. What about the female speaker? A suit still connotes the most authority for a female. However, a dress and jacket combination and tailored dresses are becoming more acceptable in some speaking scenarios. If a dress is worn, a long-sleeve rather than a short-sleeve garment is recommended. A comfortable length should also be selected for the dress or skirt. Again, the best rule is to refer to the particular situation, and dress accordingly.

Men's suits are designed to be buttoned while speaking, whereas most women's jackets are not. Once again, depending upon the level of formality, the speaker may or may not want to button the jacket. White shirts are frequently a dress favorite of men for formal occasions. However, if the speaker will be on television or filmed, a white shirt should be avoided because of the "bounce light" created by the bright lights.

It is possible to become overly focused on this aspect of nonverbal communication. Ultimately, the best suggestion is to let common sense prevail, balancing the three factors—personal look, situation, and audience.

The Peripherals

It is a good idea to empty stuffed pockets. A speaker does not need to be fiddling with eye glasses once the speech has started. If glasses are not needed during the delivery process, don't take them to the speaking platform. Leave the pocket organizer and pens at the table. Remove jingling change or key rings from pockets, as these are likely to add distracting noises to the communication process. A speaker doesn't want to sound like a U-Haul truck moving across the stage or, worse yet, look like one.

Accessories should blend rather than draw attention. Glittery jewelry, worn on a man or a woman, catches the light. This poses problems if the speaker is under a spotlight or being filmed for television or being videotaped. Dangling jewelry can produce the same problem; large bracelets that "clunk" on a podium provide extraneous noise that is accentuated near a microphone. For that reason, jewelry should be selected carefully.

Hair must be well groomed. A speaker with long hair should secure it, in order to avoid the temptation to "fiddle with one's locks." Make-up should complement a speaker's features and never appear garish. If the speaker is aware the speaking platform is under lights, a dusting of loose powder, for a male or female, is recommended.

Finally, the speaker must ask, "Am I comfortable?" If heels are "too" high or if the shirt is "too" starched, it distracts the speaker. Only the speaker can determine what clothing offers comfort, so a good coach must keep this in mind when making recommendations.

THE SPEAKER'S HANDBOOK

A speaker's handbook is an excellent addition to any speaker bureau. This book serves as a reminder for the experienced speaker and is a convenient resource for the novice. Some of the material already mentioned, such as appropriate dress and what to say during a question-and-answer session, are suitable topics for such a publication. An overview of verbal and nonverbal considerations can be listed, too. Other suggested topics follow.

Issue a Food Warning

Tips regarding food and drink are helpful. For example, a light meal may soothe the "anxious stomach," whereas a heavy meal may make a speaker sluggish. Avoiding caffeine is critical to some speakers, as drinking too much coffee or too many soft drinks produce jitters, adding to the speaker's level of anxiety.

Just as caffeine provides an unwanted jolt to the system, tranquilizing medications probably are not the best solution for speech anxiety. When tranquilizers are introduced into the system, a speaker runs the risk of muddling through a presentation with less energy and responsiveness than may be necessary.

Since drinking a very cold beverage can tighten the vocal cords, it is best to limit one's intake to warm liquids. Dairy products are known to "coat" the throat, so speakers should avoid eating ice cream or a creamed soup if a meal is served prior to the presentation.

Get the Point

At times, a speaker may use a pointer. The handbook lists guidelines for the use of this tool that include:

- Use a pointer to make a quick visual reference. If using a laser pointer, turn it off when not in use.
- Don't play with the pointer when it is not being used. It may even be appropriate to simply set the object down. However, leaving the pointer on a lighted overhead can draw significant and unnecessary attention to the prop.
- If using a laser pointer, try circling the information on the screen or use some movement. Otherwise, the laser is likely to emphasize a trembling hand.

Always on Stage

The handbook is also a good location to emphasize the ambassadorial role of the speaker. Offer suggestions to accentuate the positive image of the nonprofit being represented. It is also important to be contagious with enthusiasm.

AUDIOVISUAL AIDS

Audiovisual aids support presentations in three ways:

1. By helping to enhance audience understanding.
2. By increasing the level of audience interest.
3. By improving speaker credibility.

First ask, "Will a visual aid enhance the communication process?" If the answer is "no," it is best not to waste resources developing one. If the response is positive, the next step is to determine which visual aid provides the most support and best illustrates the message.

Before finalizing the decision of what type of visual aid to create, take into account three other considerations. First, what are the most frequent type of environments in which the speech will be delivered? Second, how comfortable will speakers bureau participants be with this type of visual aid? Third, the focus of the speech should not be on how many or how sophisticated the audiovisual aids are; the focus must be on the message. By using this premise as the guiding principle, the most appropriate and correct number of visual materials can be developed.

What are possible visual aids? The following list indicates the many options:

- photographs, illustrations, and maps
- graphs and charts
- flip charts
- slides, transparencies, filmstrips, or PowerPoint presentations
- videotapes and films
- records and tapes
- models or actual objects
- chalkboard drawings
- people
- handouts

Preparing Visual Aids

Regardless of the type of audiovisual material, there are rules to follow when creating visual aids. The primary principle is to keep everything as simple as possible. Many times, the simplest visuals communicate most effectively. Cluttering a visual usually makes it difficult to read. Creating extensive graphics, copying comprehensive financial pages, or including nonessential material suggests a novice designer.

Each visual should include a "manageable amount" of information: not so much material as to cause information overload, but also not such minimal content that the audience is unable to grasp the key point (s). The content of each slide or transparency should be limited to fifteen to twenty words. [46]

If writing appears on the visual aid, be sure that the point size of the type can be read from the back of the room. "Write big!" cannot be stressed frequently enough, as the material must be visible to the entire audience. Flip charts and posters must have extremely large lettering, measuring a minimum of 2 inches. The recommended type sizes for a PowerPoint presentation are 44 point for titles; 32 point for subtitles; and 28 point for text. [47]

Of course, thicker lettering is more visible than lettering constructed of thinner lines. A combination of uppercase and lowercase letters improves readability over the use of all uppercase. Serif types, such as Garamond, Times Roman, or Century, are generally considered easier to read in longer passages, as the serifs take the eye from one letter to the next. Most designers agree that no more than two typefaces should be used on a single visual. [48]

Pictorials enhance audience understanding. Graphics, charts, and tables offer information at a glance that might otherwise take a long time to describe. With computer-generated graphics, images are even easier to utilize and prove to be powerful tools. In fact, whether explaining a strategic plan for an organization or showing the layout plans for a new Girl Scout camp, the use of imagery greatly enhances the communication process. Using visual language leaves nothing to chance. Rather than verifying the mental images of the audience, visual communication clarifies specifics, reducing the chance for miscommunication as well.

In fact, one of the most deeply entrenched paradigms is equating communication with words. [49] Yet with cultural differences and the wide variety of individuals represented in today's audience, pictorial usage and visual organization patterns cut across many communication barriers. Any pictorial should be large enough for persons in the back row to see clearly.

The addition of color to a visual aid adds excitement and interest. Color is 32 percent more likely to attract audience attention than a black and white visual. [50] Color highlights, signals significance, or reinforces an idea through association.

Color must be contrasted to ensure readability. For example, yellow type on a white background or navy type on a black background should not be used, as they are difficult to read. The use of numerous colors on a single visual creates a "busy" look, causing the audience to be confused about where to focus. Grouping related information onto a single visual enables the audience to grasp key concepts as well as to understand the connection that exists among the various points.

If the speech has a theme, it should be incorporated into the visual aspect of the presentation. It might be appropriate to write the theme, in some form, on each visual or to specifically link speech wording to the theme. A basic color, graphic, or design scheme provides continuity for the audience, too. However, simple repetition can become boring.

Balance is another design feature. To achieve balance, sufficient space must be left around and between items. Wide margins, equal on both sides, create a feel of consistency and balance. If only a few words are used in a visual, the information is centered. An alternative is to place the material off-center but to balance it with a graphic. Columns, rows, and bullets are arranged to add organization as well as readability and balance. [51]

Tips for Using Audiovisual Materials

Only through practice can a speaker feel comfortable using this material. When helping a speaker practice, the coach should be sure to remind the speaker of the following:

- Check audiovisual equipment in advance of the presentation. Have an extra bulb for the projector or overhead.
- What lighting options are available in the room? Can the speaker assign someone to dim the lights?

- Refrain from distributing handouts during the presentation. If the audience is to follow along, material should be distributed in advance. Or pass out material at the completion of the presentation to prevent listeners from turning attention away from the speaker and toward the distribution of the handouts.
- Watch body position and movement as it relates to the speaking platform and use of any type of visual aid   (see Figure 4.2). Do not stand or walk in front of the screen upon which visuals are being projected. Do not angle the body so much toward a flip chart, poster, or other visual that it limits interaction with the audience.
- Be sure to explain the visual aid. Do not simply place the visual in the front of the room and forget to utilize it.
- Have recordings, videos, or similar materials properly cued, so the timing of a delivery is not destroyed.
- Feel comfortable with the visual. If a demonstration is involved, practice the steps several times to guarantee a smooth and well-paced presentation.
- Plan ahead for Murphy's Law. If relying on technology, have a backup plan in place should an equipment failure occur.

FINDING THE OPPORTUNITY

With speeches written, speakers in place, and support materials ready, the speakers bureau is now ready to respond to requests as well as to be marketed. The components discussed in this section include marketing, tracking, and evaluating the bureau.

Marketing

A helpful marketing tool is a speakers bureau brochure. This pamphlet describes available presentations. Information about the nonprofit is included. Speakers, particularly if well-known in the area, are listed by name. This link to personal speaker credibility acts as an additional draw. If names are specified, a brief background, including speaker qualifications or affiliations, is appropriate. Of course, contact information is imperative, so the recipient of the brochure knows how to make scheduling arrangements.

FIGURE 4.2. Positions of the Speaker and a Visual Aid

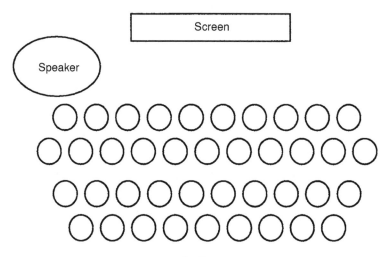

Although the brochure may be distributed in person or at meetings, it also can be used as a direct mail item. In this case, a letter may accompany the pamphlet. The correspondence can emphasize particular topics that carry critical messages for the organization's objectives. If speeches feature subjects currently being covered in the news media, these topics are highlighted, drawing special attention to them. During a crisis, the letter points out speeches added to the bureau's offerings. A suggestion that this subject matter is particularly timely can be strategically helpful to the nonprofit.

A reply form or postcard, self-addressed for easy correspondence, is tucked into the mailing. This makes the booking process easier, if the request is made via mail. A form should be kept by the telephone (see Form 4.1) to expedite call-in requests. Information that must be collected includes:

- Name of the organization requesting the speaker (and possibly the nature of the organization).
- Organization's contact person and telephone number.
- The specific program and/or speaker requested.

- Date and time requested.
- Location of speaking engagement.
- Size of anticipated audience.
- Room considerations.
- Audiovisual options.
- If videotaping arrangements can be made.

Brochures and direct mailings are very expensive. Therefore, neither of these tactics should be used unless a strategic marketing approach is taken. It is in the best interest of the nonprofit to identify audiences critical to the organization's success and to keep in mind the objectives of the nonprofit. For example, is an audience filled with government officials and decision makers who impact legislation? Or are listeners likely to volunteer time or talent?

If the nonprofit does not already have a database of community organizations, the town's chamber of commerce frequently has a comprehensive list of such groups. In most cases, the chamber offers this information free of charge to nonprofits. However, a fee may be collected, especially if the list is in the form of printed labels. Either way, the nonprofit takes the base list, prioritizes contacts, and develops a strategy to contact and follow up with these select groups.

Other public relations tactics include news releases and public service announcements (PSAs). Both vehicles are used to announce that the nonprofit has a speakers bureau. Whether using the format of a news release or a PSA, it is critical for "the basics" to be communicated, including the name of the organization, subject areas, and a telephone number that can be called to schedule a speaker.

After the initial announcement is made, PSAs can continue to remind the public about this valuable service. These subsequent public service announcements can focus on recently added topics, timely subject matters, or theme-related speeches. Please note: when determining if news releases, public service announcements, or any other public relations tactic should be used separately—or in combination—to promote the speakers bureau, the practitioner must select the promotional methods that will work best within the community.

FORM 4.1. Speaker Bureau Request Form

Information taken by: _____ Date of call: _____

Organization requesting speaker: _____

Name of contact person: _____

Telephone number of contact: (W) _____ (H) _____

Mailing address for organization: _____

_____

Date of speaking engagement: _____

Length of presentation requested: _____

Location of event: _____

Directions to location: _____

_____

_____

Audience size: _____

Topic or type of speech requested: _____

If specific speaker requested, name of individual: _____

Special material or equipment needed: _____

Equipment supplied by organization: _____

Suggested speaker: _____ Date contacted: _____

Response: _____

Suggested speaker: _____ Date contacted: _____

Response: _____

The Confirmation

After a speaker is "booked," a letter is sent to the sponsor confirming details such as date, time, topic, presentation length, and materials (see Form 4.2). Special requests, such as a lavaliere microphone, podium, or VCR, should be listed as well.

The confirmation mailing includes a brief biography of the speaker, or better yet, provides a suggested introduction. Not only does this approach make it easier for the person who introduces the program, but it also ensures that the nonprofit's desired message is communicated during initial remarks.

A copy of the request form is supplied to the speaker following confirmation of the appointment. Special arrangements or details are shared at this time, allowing the speaker adequate preparation time. The representative from the bureau follows up, reminding the speaker of the commitment. (See Form 4.3.)

FORM 4.2. Speaker Confirmation Form

Date:

To: (contact name and requesting organization)

From: (speaker bureau contact name and name of nonprofit)

Thank you for requesting a speaker from (name of nonprofit). We are pleased to supply your organization with a presentation on (subject matter). (Speaker name) will address your group on (date) at (time) at (location).

The presentation is approximately (length of speech) minutes. [Use the next sentence only if appropriate.] The following special arrangements are required: (slide projector, lavaliere microphone, VCR, etc.)

After our speaker has made (his or her) presentation, please complete the enclosed program evaluation form. It is only through such feedback that we can continue to provide topics that are relevant and speakers who are effective. Although the form will take a few minutes to complete, we appreciate your time and any input that you can offer.

We are pleased to have the opportunity to tell your group more about our organization. If I can be of further assistance or if anything has changed from our original conversation, please contact me at (telephone number).

FORM 4.3. Speaker Reminder Form

Date:

To: (speaker name and address)

From: (speaker bureau contact name)

Just a reminder that you agreed to speak to (name of organization) on (date) at (time).

The presentation location is (address). Directions to this location are (specific location instructions).

The topic of your speech is (identify which topic), and you will be addressing approximately (number) people.

[Add the following paragraph if materials such as handouts, slides, video-tapes, transparencies, etc. are required.]

Please contact (appropriate name), located at (address), to pick up all necessary materials for your speech assignment.

Should you have any questions or if a problem arises that will not permit you to fulfill this assignment, please contact me at (telephone number).

Thank you for helping (name of nonprofit) get our word out to the community!

Publicizing the Event

In many cases, the group using the speaker promotes the speaker and topic. The sponsoring organization typically mentions the upcoming event in a newsletter or at the meeting prior to the presentation. The group also may send a meeting notice to the local newspaper mentioning the featured guest. However, to maximize the promotional opportunities, the nonprofit also may opt to publicize the speaking engagement.

A news release and/or media alerts announcing the speech and speaker provide detail and invite the news media to attend the event. Before issuing such an invitation, however, it is important to check with the hosting group. In most cases, the sponsor appreciates the possibility of additional publicity. Each speaker should complete an information sheet, so material is available for publicity purposes. (See Form 4.4.)

FORM 4.4. Speaker Information Form

Date: _____

Name: _____

Telephone: (W) _____ (H) _____

Mailing address: _____

_____

Please provide information that describes your affiliation with the organization. The material located in this section of the form will be released to the media and used for promotional purposes. Please feel free to attach a resume in addition to responding to the following questions:

Experience with the organization: _____

_____

_____

_____

Positions/offices held with the organization: _____

_____

_____

Education and training: _____

_____

Current community involvement: _____

_____

_____

_____

Related awards or recognition: _____

_____

Previous volunteer experience: _____

_____

_____

Areas of interest: _____

_____

Briefly describe your public speaking experience: _____

_____

_____

After the speech, a follow-up news release or a telephone call is made to the media if major announcements were made during the speech or if the news was time-sensitive. In such cases, a copy of the speech accompanies the release. When packaging this material, a cover sheet is added. The accompanying news release highlights the major facts and the key points.

If a release and copy of the speech are sent prior to the event, it is important to use an embargo date on the news release, instructing the media to hold specific comments regarding speech content until after the engagement.

Any attending media representatives receive copies of the speech at the meeting. This reduces the chance of a misquote and makes the reporting job easier for the news representative. A listener may even request a copy. This provides another opportunity to communicate the nonprofit's message and may even produce another speaking engagement.

The Speaking Environment

Advance knowledge of the speaking environment is crucial to speaker preparation. Questions regarding the environment are asked during the booking process. In some cases, an environmental analysis is required by a speakers bureau representative. A different room arrangement may even be requested of the hosting group.

Environmental considerations include:

- Arrangement of the furniture.
- Audience seating arrangement.
- Availability of podium.
- Type of microphone (stationary or lavaliere), if any.
- Lighting (overall lighting, light at podium, ability to dim certain portions of room).
- Audiovisual equipment (type, availability, technician on site).
- Number of people expected.
- Size and location of speaking area (auditorium stage, raised platform, behind a dinner table).

THE FOLLOW-UP

Follow-up is a necessity. A telephone call to the contact from the sponsoring organization permits a bureau representative to access firsthand information regarding how the speaker and the program were received. This contact reveals the success or failure of the program. An opportunity also exists to inquire if this individual usually schedules speakers and, if so, what upcoming speaking opportunities might arise.

The second step in the follow-up process is a formal thank-you note to the primary contact and/or to the president of the host group. This demonstrates appreciation for the chance to share information about the nonprofit and displays courtesy and respect for the host organization.

Did It Work?

The effectiveness of a bureau is only improved if this question is posed after every speaking engagement. The success or failure of a presentation is determined in a variety of ways. Regardless of the specific approach taken, two steps ensure the successful continuation of speakers bureau. First, feedback is collected. Then, data is reviewed, evaluated, and shared.

For example, it may be possible to videotape the speaker. The coach then can share the tape with the speaker and discuss how the presentation can improve. Subsequent practice sessions permit the speaker to integrate the delivery suggestions into his or her performance.

An evaluation form supplied to the audience provides insight about whether the program was appropriate and met expectations, defines how well the speaker was received, and reveals audience willingness to listen to another speaker from the nonprofit   (see Form 4.5). Based on such input, decisions are made to add more topics to the speakers bureau, change an angle that is explored in the content of a speech, provide additional coaching for a speaker, or contact the sponsoring group with other program ideas.

Checking media response is a must, either through coverage of the event or the generation of follow-up features on the nonprofit. Media publicity increases the effectiveness of the bureau because

FORM 4.5. Speaker Bureau Program Evaluation Form

Please answer the following questions. Your input will help us maintain a viable speakers bureau, offering topics and speakers of interest to your group and others in the community. After you complete this form, please return it in the enclosed reply envelope at your earliest possible convenience. Thank you for your assistance.

Name of organization: _____

Date of speech: _____

Location: _____

Topic: _____

Speaker's name: _____

1. The presentation was:
   (circle one)   excellent   good   fair   poor

2. The presentation satisfied your group's needs?
   (circle one)   yes   no

3. The speaker was:
   (circle one)   excellent   good   fair   poor

4. How would you rate the audience's response to this presentation?
   (circle one)   excellent   good   fair   poor

5. Was the speech informative?
   (circle one)   yes   no

6. Was the content related to the topic?
   (circle one)   yes   no

7. Would you recommend this speaker to others?
   (circle one)   yes   no

8. May we release your comments?
   (circle one)   yes   no

9. What would have made this presentation more effective? _____
   _____
   _____

10. Please list other topics or subject areas that would be of interest to your group.
   _____
   _____

the size of the audience is automatically expanded due to increased visibility about the event.

Close monitoring of the bureau identifies which organizations rely on the speakers bureau for programs, determines if audience target objectives are met, and measures how the audiences responded. For example, is there a correlation between the number of new volunteers and the increased number of people exposed to the nonprofit through the bureau? Or did the amount of donations increase? If so, what percent of this figure is linked to the speakers bureau?

To be truly effective, the evaluation process must be an ongoing effort, creating a constant feedback loop. Such an approach permits the bureau to add relevant topics, to delete stale subject matter, to offer pertinent coaching advice to speakers, to strategically select speaking engagements, and to maximize the effectiveness of the speakers bureau.

Volunteer Thank You

Another critical component in the follow-up process is thanking the volunteer. Practicing and delivering a speech is a time-consuming task. Demonstrating an appreciation for these efforts will not go unnoticed.

How can a volunteer be thanked? Common courtesy dictates that a thank-you note is written to the individual speaker. In some cases, sending a copy of the note or a separate thank-you letter to a boss, parent, or other appropriate person provides additional recognition and can garner future support for this particular activity.

Another way to thank speakers is to demonstrate the value of their opinions and desire to continue to improve the program based on feedback provided by bureau participants. Therefore, ask presenters how they believe the speakers bureau can be improved, incorporate valuable suggestions, and update volunteers on the changes.

Public recognition is an excellent way to say "thank you" as well as to motivate for future participation. For example, a feature article in the nonprofit's newsletter can tout the hard work and dedication of speakers and how this helps the organization achieve its goals. After a speaker has delivered a specific number of presentations, some memento, such as a certificate or coffee mug, can be bestowed. The gift need not be large. It is the thought that counts.

RECAP

Several steps are involved in creating and maintaining an effective speakers bureau. Perhaps the easiest way to progress through the development and ongoing bureau efforts is to review each component in the following checklist:

1. Determine the purpose of the speakers bureau.
2. Establish a basic structure for the program, including promotion, the scheduling process, and evaluation.
3. Select appropriate themes and topics, compatible with the objectives of the nonprofit.
4. Write speeches and develop presentations.
5. Recruit speakers.
6. Train speakers.
7. Follow up on the activity through confirmation and evaluation.
8. Thank speakers.
9. Measure bureau results and continuously improve the program to meet objectives.

Chapter 5

The Board of Directors: Selection, Development, and Succession Planning

With the debate over public funding, a reduction in governmental financial support, and the increasing number of nonprofits competing for private donations, it is crucial for boards of directors to reexamine how they govern themselves and manage their resources.

> A decade ago, a strong director and a competent staff could create a first-class institution and raise money to support it with minimal assistance from trustees. It is next to impossible to do that today. Success depends on the combined efforts of the director, staff, and board. Even the most seasoned administrators cannot succeed without the support and hard work of a proactive board. . . . [N]ew circumstances necessitate focused and knowledgeable board performance if the institutions are to achieve their mission and reach full potential. . . . [T]rustees are most successful when they have a clear understanding of their role in fulfilling an agency's mission . . . . Formal training, followed by mission review and strategic planning, is the best way to move forward. [1]

This quotation attests to the fact that nonprofits can no longer be content with simply finding "a warm body" to fill a board seat or asking someone who will likely accept when asked. The quotation also suggests that boards consisting of "name-only" members—people who lend their names to an organization without taking an active role in the management or fund-raising activities of the nonprofit—will not be able to survive in the future. Although both of these scenarios have worked in the past, such methods fail to produce strong boards capable of survival today. Instead, a strategic approach, focused on the organization's future and clearly identifying the type of board membership it takes to achieve the organization's goal, is critical. Business has long used this approach. Nonprofits must change their course to adopt this strategic methodology.

For most nonprofits to adhere to this businesslike approach, attitudinal and cultural changes are necessary. The nonprofit's executive director must be the driving force in this effort, assuming the official responsibilities for recruitment and development of the board. Only if this duty rests with the highest ranking employee can the assignment receive the attention it deserves. To further support this endeavor and because the organization's public relations team will interact with board members and become involved with board issues, the PR director will likely assist with recruiting and training board members.

A CLOSER LOOK AT THE NONPROFIT

Before recruitment and development of board members begins, the agency itself must be examined. The board type must be identified: trade or professional association, civic club, educational institution or local school board, church or religious group, city council, state government, foundation board, hospital, museum, arts agency, youth-centered club, health or human service organization, or advisory group.

Next, the nonprofit's governance style, philosophical beliefs, mission, and objectives are clarified. Criteria for board members is established and distinct standards for board performance measurement is developed. A model is then structured, creating specific nomination guidelines.

Typically, board governance adheres to a basic organizational pattern with clearly identified responsibilities of policy-setting, fiscal guidance and use of funds, ongoing management, public accountability, and the periodic review of the nonprofit's policies, programs, and operations. [2] Also, the board ensures the organization meets its standards, not simply in an evaluative capacity, but through full achievement. [3]

What is the organization's philosophy, and how does adherence to these principles personify the group?

> The essence of any organization lies in what it believes, what it stands for, and what and how it values. . . . These values and perspectives form the bedrock on which the more mechanical and visible aspects of an organization are based. . . . [V]alues dominate policies that are instructive to staff, that is, policies that notify the staff what to do or not to do. . . . Because policies permeate and dominate all aspects of organizational life, they present the most powerful lever for the exercise of leadership. [4]

By clarifying the nonprofit's principles regarding board governance and philosophical ideals, the nonprofit's leadership needs are better matched with the qualifications of potential board members. Candidates' backgrounds and management styles are checked to ensure compatibility with the nonprofit.

As the candidate recommendation and selection process proceeds, it is common for the nonprofit to consider its unique history and "personality." In turn, this perception is frequently considered when discussing candidate personalities. Despite the belief regarding an organization's uniqueness, the focus cannot be on the board's peculiarities or the history of the group, nor can a candidate be discounted because the individual's persona does not automatically match with the group's "established personality." Instead, concentration rests with the type of individual needed to strategically lead the organization to achieve its mission and long-term goals. [5] The focus is on the future success of the nonprofit in the highly dynamic and ever-changing environment in which it operates.

WHO VOLUNTEERS?

It is necessary to discuss who volunteers. Volunteering increased slightly from 1993 to 1995. Individuals offered an estimated 20.3 billion hours in volunteer time in 1995, up from 19.5 billion in 1993. This is an average of 4.2 hours per week, per volunteer. [6] Forty-eight percent of the population—a total of 93 million people—volunteered in 1995, with a value of $201.5 billion. [7]

Closer examination of this data reveals that volunteerism is increasing in the following demographic categories: non-whites, African Americans, Hispanics, persons between twenty-five and thirty-four years old, those with household income between $75,000 and $100,000, Catholics, those with no religious affiliation, and the unemployed. According to statistics gathered in May 1996, volunteerism also increased in both gender categories. Declining volunteerism, registering at a level of 5 percent or greater, was seen in the eighteen-to-twenty-four-year-old age group and in the annual income brackets of $20,000 to $30,000 and $30,000 to $40,000. [8]

Such demographic information is helpful, because it cues those developing the list of possible board nominees to realize the large pool of eligible candidates from which to draw. Consequently, emphasis is placed on what motivates the targeted group to contribute personal time to nonprofit commitment.

In *Marketing for Nonprofit Organization* s, David Rados summarized the reasons for volunteerism: the volunteer work was useful, fun, and benefited someone the individual knew. [9] Observation of positive role models in volunteer activities and family member participation in these efforts also influence an individual's volunteerism as an adult. In fact, according to *Giving and Volunteering in the United States* (1996), 78.4 percent of the respondents took their cue to volunteer from witnessing a family member do so. [10] All of these factors are stronger than other motivators such as the thought of learning new skills or having a great deal of free time. [11]

Schindler-Rainman and Lippitt identified two trends in volunteerism. Their findings suggest that volunteers are more demanding, because they want greater input into what they are doing rather than simply filling the role of a drone in a large enterprise. Secondly, others challenge the desirability of volunteerism from a financial standpoint. According to this study, unions are concerned that paid employment opportunities are reduced through volunteerism. Also, because women filled the majority of volunteer positions in the past, other groups feel that volunteerism perpetuates the notion that women's labor is not valuable if unpaid. [12] The latter discussion, of course, cannot be as strongly considered as in the past, since the level of volunteerism among males is rising.

Another emerging trend indicates that people are more likely to be involved with multiple causes. [13] The proportion of individuals donating time to more than one organization increased a full percentage point between 1993 and 1995. [14] Consequently, people should not be discounted as board candidates if they are already volunteers. In fact, a person demonstrating volunteer spirit is more likely to accept director responsibilities than someone who is not actively involved in a volunteer effort.

SELECTING THE CANDIDATES

To narrow the large field of possible board candidate, it is best to specify selection criteria. Typically, board responsibilities include:

- Help to define the mission and purpose of the nonprofit.
- Select the senior executive and review his or her performance.
- Ensure sound organizational plans are in place and adequate resources available.
- Ensure assets are preserved and managed effectively.
- Monitor performance of the nonprofit's programs.
- Improve the organization's image.
- Assess board performance.
- Serve as a court of appeals for management problems. [15]
- Lend executive support.
- Establish a clear board role. [16]

Directors must possess a wide variety of characteristics such as effective interpersonal skills, honesty, financial expertise, conscientiousness, an awareness of social responsibility, objectivity, intelligence, common sense, and courage to act. However, it is difficult to find all of the aforementioned characteristics in a single board member. Therefore, the board, as a whole, must reflect these traits. [17] For this reason, it is particularly important to carefully research each candidate, identifying strengths and screening for needed attributes to supplement a current or impending board weakness.

Review of potential board members includes the following evaluation criteria:

- Personal skills, talents, and interests
- Affiliations and reputation
- Willingness to raise funds
- Diversity

Personal Skills, Talents, and Interests

The nominating committee, current board members, or the organization's staff generally identify board candidates. Regardless of the origin of the submission, the nominating committee thoroughly examines the individual's credentials before asking the person to assume a board role.

In many cases, the PR officer participates in the background check. For example, the public relations department may design a referral form for prospective board members and maintain a referral bank of board candidates (see Form 5.1). The PR department also assembles particulars such as a record of the person's donation history, profession, ethnic background, geographic location of residence, employer, and volunteer history with the nonprofit. If the candidate is already a volunteer with the group, the nonprofit conducts an internal check to determine if the individual expressed an interest in greater involvement within the organization or mentioned a desire to try new assignments. Articulating a willingness to donate more time to the nonprofit is crucial, as the task of being an involved board member is extremely time-consuming.

Although not easy to accomplish, informal research must be conducted to decide if the candidate accepts responsibility and follows through on commitments. Another area to investigate is how strongly the individual acts as an advocate for the needs and concerns of the organizations he or she supports. [18] Of particular importance are the willingness to welcome information and advice, to respect the right of others to disagree, and to accept decisions made by the majority voice—even when against personal conviction—and lend support to those decisions. [19]

Relationships with staff are also an issue. Board and staff must be able to work together with a mutual appreciation of abilities and talents both have to offer. Is the candidate likely to treat staff as faceless, menial workers? Or does the individual acknowledge a quality performance by paid personnel? Is the candidate likely to

FORM 5.1. Board of Directors Candidate Form

Submitted/Sponsored by: _____ Date: _____

Name of candidate: _____

Home address: _____

Home telephone: _____ Work telephone: _____

Business address (if different): _____

Occupation and job title: _____

Education/training: _____
_____

Honors and awards: _____

Organizations/affiliations: _____
_____
_____

Current charitable activities in which he or she is involved: _____
_____
_____

Possible interest level in this nonprofit: _____
_____

Possible organizational activities in which he or she would be particularly interested in becoming involved: _____
_____
_____

Would he or she be likely to participate in fund-raising? If so, in what way?
_____
_____

Your personal recommendation regarding this candidate: _____
_____
_____

report through staff when appropriate? Or will ego preclude such a possibility? Worse yet, is it likely that the prospective board member would investigate a problem by talking with a lower-level staff member or instigate dissension among personnel? [20]

The level of board interest impacts staff morale and, ultimately, the success of the nonprofit. Is the candidate likely to participate in special events or attend functions? Does the candidate demonstrate initiative by making fund-raising contacts and networking for the nonprofit? Or does the prospective member appear shy about such activities? Is the candidate likely to spread the organization's message at a personal level, creating enthusiasm and motivating others to "hop on the bandwagon"? [21] The willingness to share talents and professional expertise is a desirable trait in a candidate. Broad-based, practical skills are required as well. [22]

The public relations pro tactfully gathers all of the information, which enables the nominating committee to make an initial determination regarding the candidate's qualifications and ability to fulfill board requirements. The process involves telephone calls, informal interviews, direct observation, and research through community and professional organizations. Compiled information is forwarded to the nominating committee.

After a review of this data, the nominating committee determines if further background data are necessary to qualify the candidate for a current opening or if the person should be considered at a later point in time.

Affiliations and Reputation

In addition to the demographic data, other information, such as the degree of personal influence the candidate possesses, is examined. Some nonprofit programs only succeed if their message is communicated to the "right" audience. Board members play a significant role in this process, [23] working as catalysts to influence those who can assist the nonprofit achieve its goals. Here, again, the public relations professional generally assists in the research efforts.

Answers to the following questions must be explored:

- What are the civic organizations with which the candidate is affiliated?

- Does the person have any ties with local, state, or federal government?
- What type of reputation does the person have in the community (a "go-getter," a leader, a successful fund-raiser)?
- Will the person have credibility as a public speaker?
- Would affiliations or reputation qualify this candidate for key posts on the board?

Even if the committee decides not to nominate the candidate, such background remains on file with the public relations department. The file is confidential but available for use the next time a board opening occurs.

Willingness to Raise Funds

For directors, fund-raising poses a dual responsibility. One is to help manage the funds, including the cost of paying for fund-raising. Managing the cost to raise funds addresses such issues as hiring professional fund-raisers, and the cost of direct mail appeals, special events, and telemarketing activities. [24]

The second function is to identify new funding sources and personally assist in raising money. This assignment assumes several forms. For example, the potential candidate may have relationships with individuals, companies, or organizations likely to support the nonprofit. In this case, the board member identifies potential donors, makes the actual request for contribution, or both. Perhaps the candidate has the expertise and is willing to spearhead a major fund-raising effort or chair a special event.

The willingness to offer personal financial support to the organization is of equal importance. As P. Burke Keegan, in *Fundraising for Nonprofits* , explains: "Writing a check is an important part of real commitment. I believe it's called 'putting your money where your mouth is.' " [25]

The issue isn't that each board member contribute the same amount of money, that those with fewer discretionary funds mortgage a home to secure a high contribution, or that monied board members aren't asked to make a large donation. In fact, the issue is not how much an individual gives; rather, the issue is that every board member has a financial obligation to support the nonprofit.

"Put quite simply, everyone who serves on a board of trustees must contribute some cash every year to his or her organization. How much they contribute is another matter, but there should be no ambiguity about the requirement of some sort of annual cash gift." [26] If all members contribute, the integrity of the board increases when it approaches the community with its fund-raising efforts and requests financial support from others, because the board itself has supported the organization.

It is not unusual for a potential funder to ask, "What percentage of your trustees contribute to your organization?" If 100 percent of the trustees are contributing and if 20 percent of the total money raised by individuals comes from the board, the donor sees a level of commitment. [27]

Consequently, the nonprofit must scrutinize a candidate's past financial support. Although it seems self-serving, it is imperative the candidate's giving history demonstrates financial support. While examining this data, the organization also should consider how likely it is that the candidate will increase the level of giving. Checks throughout the community yield additional information such as if the candidate sponsored other activities, underwrote a project, or was identified as a patron.

Because of the sensitivity of personal finance, it is critical this information is gathered by the public relations professional in the strictest of confidence and shared only with appropriate individuals. Indiscreet handling of such information jeopardizes future monetary donations and results in the loss of active volunteers.

Diversity

In this section, the term "diversity" is not limited to ethnic or cultural background. Although this is certainly one interpretation, the word is meant to imply a broader connotation. In addition to the aforementioned aspects, board diversity is reflected through factors such as age, gender, political convictions, educational background, profession, and socioeconomic status. Previous experiences, other affiliations, and location of residences contribute to the diversity mix as well. [28]

Such information is obtained through research or directly from the individual. Either way, these key dimensions must be considered when creating a well-rounded board that typifies the community or area it represents and serves.

Completing the Grid

After collecting this data, the nominating committee completes a chart or grid that distinguishes the skills and qualities possessed by each current and potential board member. (See Figure 5.1.) Once this step is completed, the committee compares this chart with the qualities identified as being necessary for an effective board of directors. By analyzing and contrasting the data from both grids, the strongest candidates become apparent.

Each candidate is reviewed in regard to individual talents and skills as well as from a diversity standpoint. This ensures that diversity is maximized at the board level and assignments do not emphasize minority representation. In fact, responsibility is aligned with individual ability rather than minority status or diversity issues. [29]

As the grid is reviewed, it becomes apparent where "holes" or "weak links" are. Special care is taken to select individuals who reflect the needed attributes and are likely to be dedicated to the organization and its mission.

If other organizations within the community maintain membership reflective of particular characteristics, one option is to contact these organizations for nominee suggestions. For example, the local bar association may know of attorneys willing to contribute time and offer services free of charge. Or the local chapter of the NAACP may suggest a member who is interested in greater community involvement. Leaders at local churches can identify individuals who meet the required criteria. Such resources are extremely helpful in locating volunteers who represent a cross section of the community and reflect the talents and skills necessary for a well-rounded board of directors.

Recruiting individuals of various backgrounds yields two benefits:

- An increased likelihood of achieving greater creativity through the synergy of diversity.
- A greater possibility of new or enhanced understanding of the nonprofit's stakeholders or clients.

Figure 5.1. Board Profile Considerations Checklist

By developing a checklist of desired characteristics, skills, and experience, it is possible to review current and prospective board members to assess strengths and identify board needs. By taking this strategic approach, existing "gaps" are filled and a strong board of directors emerges. Considerations are listed below and categorized for ease of review.

Expertise or Professional Skill

- organizational management
- financial management
- administration experience
- finance
  - ✓ accounting
  - ✓ banking, trusts
  - ✓ investments
  - ✓ insurance
- fund-raising
- law
- marketing
- personnel
- building and grounds
  - ✓ engineering
  - ✓ architecture
  - ✓ real estate
- long-range/strategic planning
- public relations
  - ✓ media
  - ✓ chamber of commerce
  - ✓ speakers bureau
- government regulations and representation
- representative of client group served by nonprofit
- special background
  - ✓ health
  - ✓ education
  - ✓ medical
- business/corporate

Age

- Under 35
- 35-49
- 50-64
- 65 or over

Gender

- male
- female

Ethnic Background

- African American
- Asian/Pacific Islander
- Hispanic
- Native American
- Caucasian

Geographical Location
(This is dependent upon area served and mission of organization.)

- international
- national
- regional
- state
- county
- city
- rural

Financial Indicators

- retired
- salaried
- hourly
- self-employed
- philanthropic reputation
- prospective major donor

Other Pertinent Data
(These personal characteristics are unique to some nonprofit boards.)

- disability
- sexual orientation
- parent
- educational level

Previous Assignments As Board Member

Current Assignments As Board Member

Potential Board Committee Responsibilities

- executive
- nominating
- program
- development/fund-raising
- finance
- audit
- building and grounds
- other

Figure 5.1 (*continued*)

Length of Previous Board Service

- more than 10 years
- 5-10 years
- 2-4 years
- fewer than 2 years

Length of Service to Nonprofit

- more than 10 years
- 5-10 years
- 2-4 years
- fewer than 2 years

Other Community Activities

- current
- past

Note: Much of this information is found in *Six Keys to Recruiting, Orienting, and Involving Nonprofit Board Members* by Judith Grummon Nelson and published by the National Center for Nonprofit Boards, 1997. The publication also has worksheets containing related material.

THE JOB DESCRIPTION

The next step is to write a job description or, if appropriate, revise an existing one. The job description clearly states what is required of the new board member. It includes the specific responsibilities and overall accountability of board membership. Such descriptions tend to be simpler than typical professional job descriptions, but even a limited list of responsibilities provides clarification. [30]

Specific time frames for agreed-upon tasks are included in this write-up. [31] For example, the development chair has a predetermined time frame for a fund-raising campaign. Identifying key assignments during recruitment, such as spearheading a committee or acting as treasurer, allows candidates to determine if they have the necessary time, talent, and interest to perform the various tasks. A job description also makes the evaluation process easier when determining if an individual should remain on the board and, if so, in what capacity. (See Figure 5.2.)

FIGURE 5.2. Sample Job Description: Board of Director's Secretary

Length of term: One year.

Purpose: To ensure that actions of the board of directors are documented and properly recorded.

Primary Responsibilities:

- Provide written agendas prior to board meetings and standing committees.

- Distribute to board members pertinent background information on subjects to be addressed at the meeting.

- Prepare and provide written minutes to board members within the time frame specified by the bylaws and procedures.

- File approved minutes as stipulated by the organization's procedures.

Normal board of director responsibilities must also be fulfilled.

A long-term expectation may be involved with a board assignment. For example, if the candidate agrees to serve in a specific capacity, does this mean the individual is in line to serve as president in two or three years? Such details are stated in the job description.

Board accountability is also addressed. Such references can be extremely complex in description or generic in nature. For example, board duties may specify that no more than three board meetings can be missed during a year and that participation in the speakers bureau is mandatory. Or the board requirements may be general, such as "be a team player" or "make time for board service." [32] Either way, the job description addresses responsibilities of the assignments, expectations, and key priorities of the individual post as well as the requirements of board membership. [33]

The nominating committee, the nonprofit's executive director, or a staff member may write the job description. The organization's trained communicator—the public relations person—can offer input to ensure the job description is concisely worded and free of organizational jargon.

With roles clearly identified and a list of approved candidates, the nominating committee matches individuals to board vacancies. [34]

RECRUITING

Who should be responsible for recruitment? The organization must determine who the best person is to make the request or if a team approach should be used. For example, if a current board member has excellent rapport with the candidate, a personal call may be the most appropriate tactic. Additionally, the president or the executive director of the nonprofit might be required to recruit a "big name."

Once the individual or team is identified, the recruiters prepare for the call. If the nominee is familiar with the organization, the specific job description and a board of directors manual may be the only materials needed. The written job description "doubles" as a discussion piece during the appointment and as a "leave behind" for the candidate to study.

The importance of a clear and succinct job description cannot be overstated. Frequently, candidates are not fully informed about the amount of work required. Presenting a precisely written description offers the candidate a chance to accept the position or decline the workload because of other responsibilities. [35] If sufficient discussion regarding time requirements occurs, an increased likelihood exists that new board members will take an active role in the organization. [36]

If the candidate is unfamiliar with the nonprofit, additional information is required. Pertinent literature includes an annual report, recent newsletter, fact sheet, and organizational brochure. These printed pieces can be used effectively during the request and left for the candidate to review. [37]

Since the public relations professional is in charge of this literature, all materials are assembled and packaged to create a professional image. A slide show or video may be necessary for the recruiting effort. If so, the PR department supplies these audiovisual items.

Since potential board members are busy, a clear agenda is provided. Suggested topics and a meeting order follow:

1. Thank the candidate for meeting.
2. Notify the individual you would like him or her to consider a board of director nomination. Acknowledge that the board makes the final decision, based on needs, skills, and diversity issues.
3. Explain your relationship to the nonprofit.
4. Provide a brief overview of the mission, history, and program of the organization. Refer to printed materials and any "leave behinds."
5. Ask if the prospective board member has any questions or comments, taking notes if necessary.
6. Answer as many questions as possible.
7. Review the job description developed for the particular board position.
8. Explain that board orientation is provided.
9. Explain that a "board partner" is available for mentoring.
10. Clearly state the number of board meetings held each year, the expectations regarding fund-raising (personal contributions and/or involvement in an annual campaign), and the required participation in committee work. (To better prepare for this discussion, see Figure 5.3.)
11. Permit time for more questions and respond to each inquiry.
12. Summarize the discussion quickly, including a "thank you" for the meeting time.
13. Invite the person to attend a meeting or an event, so the prospective member can see programs in action and meet other board members.
14. Ask if the person is willing to be nominated, reminding the individual that the board must vote on all board members. If the person agrees, require the nominee to complete a declaration of interest form. If this person needs time to make a decision, leave the form for completion and later submission. (See Form 5.2.)
15. If the person declines to serve on the board due to time commitments or other barriers, ask if the individual would consider participating in other ways, such as an advisory

board member, donor, etc. Inquire if the person would serve on the board in the future.

16. Leave the information packet about the nonprofit before you exit.[38]

Next, when and where does the recruitment occur? Will the call be made during business hours at the person's place of employment? Or will the request be made at lunch or over dinner? Will the gathering be at someone's home or in a restaurant? Whatever the decision, every effort is made to create an appropriate environment,

FIGURE 5.3. Suggestions for Successful Board Membership

- Regularly attend board and committee meetings.
- Read and understand the minutes of board meetings and the minutes of your committee assignments.
- Read your organization's publications.
- Inquire if there is something you do not understand or if something comes to your attention that causes you to question a policy or practice.
- Avoid conflict of interest issues, either fiscal or programmatic.
- Monitor the community and professional image of your organization.
- Be certain policies are clearly identified and that the board acts on them as a group rather than as a small group of individuals.
- Know your organization's board of directors, programs, and staff.
- Insist the board have a policy relative to board volunteer liability.
- Understand the difference between staff and board functions, staff and board roles, and policy and implementation.
- Recognize that staff members have other responsibilities apart from work with the board.

Note: These discussion points were taken from a comprehensive list of guidelines prepared by William R. Conrad Jr. and William E. Glenn in their book, *Effective Voluntary Board of Directors* (Athens, OH: Swallow Press, 1983).

FORM 5.2. Board of Directors Declaration of Interest

Name: _____ Date: _____

Company name: _____

Preferred mailing address: _____

Home telephone: _____ Work telephone: _____

Have you ever served on the board of this agency before? _____

Do you personally support (name of nonprofit)? _____ If so, how? _____

What personal strengths do you believe you would bring to the board? _____

_____

_____

_____

_____

Please list any leadership skills or experience you possess, particularly with other nonprofit organizations: _____

_____

_____

_____

_____

Please list any experience, personal accomplishments, or nonprofit participation you believe would qualify you for a board of director position in this organization:

_____

_____

_____

Board of director terms are for (fill in appropriate number) years. Could you serve this length of term? _____ Occasionally, a shorter appointment is available. Would you prefer a shorter term?

Please return to:
(contact name)
(name of nonprofit)
(mailing address)

so the request for board membership is accepted. Depending upon what arrangement is selected, the public relations department may assist with these plans as well.

If an answer is not provided at the time of the request, the candidate should be contacted approximately one week after the call to secure a response. [39]

WELCOME AND ORIENTATION

Success! The candidate agreed to board nomination. A vote is taken; approval is received. It's official. A new person joins the board. Now, the real work begins.

"Too many individuals are carefully wooed and placed on boards only to be left to fend for themselves to decipher their role." [40] This is primarily because nonprofits, faced with numerous time constraints, shift their focus immediately from the new board member to board business. Although this may seem expeditious, it is ineffective. The board member who feels welcome and receives training is a much greater asset than the board member who is courted and then "ignored."

The first mission is to make the new board member feel welcome. This task is likely to be handled by the executive director with the help of the public relations department or is simply assigned to the PR staff. A formal letter of welcome and acknowledgment of the new member's willingness to serve is sent. The executive director, the volunteer president, or both individuals sign the letter.   (See Form 5.3.) The public relations department also plans the formal induction ceremony for new board members and officers.

New members complete volunteer information forms   (see Form 5.4), with the understanding that the material is used for promotional purposes. Using these facts, the public relations office sends a news release to appropriate media announcing the new board member. Such recognition provides an immediate win-win opportunity as the new board member receives acknowledgment, and the nonprofit has a chance to gain positive press exposure.

The form is housed in confidential files in the public relations department. As new leadership roles are accepted, individual recognition gained, or awards earned, data in the volunteer file are up-

Form 5.3. Sample Welcome Letter to New Board Members

(Date)

Dear (name of new board member):

Welcome! We are delighted to have you as a new member of our board of directors and look forward to working with you in this capacity. We have many exciting plans for the upcoming year and are confident that your addition to the board will help us achieve these goals.

So you can get to know us better, we'd like you to join us for new member orientation that is scheduled on (date) from (starting time) to (stopping time) at (location). At this session, you will have the opportunity to meet other new board members, our officers, and staff.

The orientation agenda is enclosed. We believe you will find the session well-planned, informative, and helpful. We also encourage you to come with any questions you might have about (name or organization).

Congratulations and thank you for your willingness to serve on our board. We look forward to seeing you on (date) and working closely with you throughout your term.

Sincerely,

Executive Director

Enclosure

dated. This up-to-date information is incorporated into news releases publicizing volunteer recognition, used in introductions in public speaking scenarios, cited in the organization's newsletter, and referred to when considering identifying candidates for officer roles or committee positions.

The public relations staff is typically involved with planning a meeting for the formal induction of new board members and officers.

FORM 5.4. Confidential Board of Directors Volunteer Information Form

Name: _____

Preferred mailing address: _____

Home telephone: _____ Work telephone: _____

Fax number: _____ E-mail address: _____

Name of employer: _____ Job title: _____

Birth date: _____ Date elected to board: _____

Name of spouse: _____

Education and training: _____
_____
_____
_____

Have you had any previous involvement with this organization? _____
If yes, describe: _____
_____
_____
_____

Membership in volunteer organizations, professional associations, service clubs, or social groups. Please list any offices or chair positions you have held:
_____
_____
_____
_____
_____
_____

Political offices held: _____
_____
_____

Civic appointments: _____
_____
_____

Special awards or recognition received: _____

_____

_____

_____

_____

Hobbies and special interests: _____

_____

_____

_____

_____

Are you willing to participate in the speakers bureau? _____

Do you have any public speaking training or experience? _____

Are you available for radio programs? _____ TV shows? _____
Newspaper or magazine interviews? _____

Preferred committee assignments: _____

_____

_____

_____

_____

I have special skills/talents and would like to help (name of nonprofit) in the following ways: _____

_____

_____

_____

_____

_____

_____

For publicity purposes, please send a photograph. Otherwise, with your permission, we would like to make arrangements to have a photo taken.

If you have any questions, please contact (name) at (telephone number).

After completing this form, please return to:
(Name)
(Name of nonprofit organization)
(Mailing address)

Orientation

Although recruits received information about the nonprofit, board training still addresses the organization's purpose, services, history, and organizational structure. [41] A slide show, video, or film, available through the **PR** department, provides an excellent visual medium to illustrate the work and goals of the organization. Audiovisual material adds variety to the flow of information. [42]

Each participant receives a "Board Member Handbook." The manual or notebook contains a copy of the organization's bylaws; a copy of rules, policies, and procedures for the organization; a list of board members, including addresses and telephone numbers; a list of board officers, plus a general description of duties; organizational chairs; a list of staff members with a brief listing of individual responsibilities; a glossary of terms; a list of board meeting dates, times, and locations; [43] financial and operating reports for the past year; a copy of the nonprofit's strategic plan; a copy of the organization's liability policy; [44] current annual budget; [45] funding sources; [46] key dates for the organization, such as dates for special events or fund-raising campaigns; and the names of committee chairs and committee assignments.

When planning orientation, key personnel from the nonprofit are included. The president and executive director of the nonprofit take part in the program. Volunteer chairs and/or staff members may speak. It may even be appropriate to include a client or someone who benefits from the nonprofit. [47] The nonprofit's public relations department is on the agenda, too. During this time, the **PR** professional explains the various uses of the Volunteer Information Form, the importance of the speakers bureau, and how board members help protect and enhance the image of the nonprofit.

During orientation, new members are again encouraged to consider what is required of them. A checklist of subject areas with which the new member should be familiar by the end of the session is distributed. This encourages a self-test at the conclusion of the orientation to make sure new members have sufficient knowledge to successfully participate as productive board members. [48]

Depending upon the personality of the nonprofit and its function in society, role playing can be added to the agenda. Such a participatory exercise helps board members better understand the function that the nonprofit plays and the clients it serves.

While an overview of the purpose and structure of the nonprofit is important, it is also helpful to introduce new members to the specific programs or departments with which they will work. Consequently, "break out" sessions permit committee chairs and staff to meet with newly assigned board members. During this "learning session," it is a good idea to employ numerous media techniques and keep speeches brief to maintain a high level of interest and optimize the learning environment.

Newcomers must not be inundated with too much material, as this results in information overload. [49] If an extensive amount of material needs to be covered, a basic orientation followed by mini-seminars on key topics is one solution to keep new material introduction at a comprehendible level.

Where should the orientation be held? Obviously, it is a choice between on or off site. If held on site, a tour of the facility should be included. All members of the paid staff are easily accessible, giving the new board member a chance to immediately meet all personnel. If regular board meetings are held at the headquarters, orientation can follow a board meeting, possibly saving time for new members. However, it is highly advisable to complete the orientation process *prior* to the first board meeting.

Although holding orientation on site has many advantages, there are excellent reasons for conducting the sessions away from the main facility. A quiet, comfortable setting provides an excellent retreat from the busy office. Newcomers feel on "equal footing" with veterans. Plus, new members are likely to be less inhibited about asking questions and exploring options or opinions. [50]

Depending upon the time of day the orientation is scheduled and the length of the agenda, food and beverages are offered. Even if the session is relatively brief, light snacks and beverages should be served. This adds to the comfort level of the learning environment, making the experience more enjoyable and productive for the new board member. If the session is longer than a half-day, a meal should be arranged.

The Buddy System

To help new board members acclimate more quickly and to make these members feel part of the team, introducing a "buddy system" or a board mentoring process is helpful. In this system, a new board member is assigned to a seasoned veteran. The two individuals sit next to each other during meetings and may even ride together to board sessions. Since asking a question can be intimidating to the new board member, the question can be asked by the longtime board member. Most certainly, the veteran fills information gaps or points the new person in the proper direction to ascertain the information. [51] In fact, the experienced person is typically charged with making sure the new board member has a strong grasp of the critical issues facing the board and a solid understanding of how the board works. [52]

DEVELOPING AND RETAINING BOARD MEMBERS

Even with orientation complete, board education is far from over. In fact, it is crucial to develop members to maximum potential. Board development occurs in the same manner that people mature in their professions. By being involved and given the chance to complete tasks in a supervised setting, [53] new members feel as if they actively contribute to the success of the nonprofit while they learn more about the organization.

Additional training is offered frequently throughout the year. Because volunteers have limited time, sessions are well-organized and informative, and participants feel their time is spent in a worthwhile manner. Programs are crafted carefully for those attending the session. In fact, specifically targeted programs have a much better chance of achieving training objectives than generic ones. This is why breakout seminars or mini-seminars are extremely productive. Time is also allotted for board input. Volunteers appreciate the opportunity to comment on ideas and offer suggestions, [54] as this incorporates greater relevancy into the sessions. In some cases, outside experts offer an objective view and provide informative lectures on specific methodology to improve decision making, [55] fund-raising techniques, or strategic planning.

The best way to adhere to the strategic plan is to keep the mission of the organization in front of board members and the staff. For that reason, the mission statement should be read during training sessions.[56] While reexamining this statement, it is wise to schedule discussion time to make board members feel everything possible is being done to meet primary objectives. The public relations professional can record such information and use noteworthy examples in the newsletter.

Since the board is faced with a variety of issues, such as how to increase board diversity, highly focused discussions are an effective means for members to comment on board progress. This time also serves as an informal training session on critical topics.

If the nonprofit is affiliated with a national organization, the local chapter can take advantage of the resources offered by the parent agency. Workshops or seminars, sponsored by the national organization, are designed to assist the chapter with problem-solving, fund-raising, and long-range planning.

While the national association may offer expertise not available at the local level, former members or administrators who served on the board or worked with the local chapter are also resources. These individuals have an intimate perspective and can offer guidance not found elsewhere.

The Board Retreat

An annual, well-planned board retreat is one component of an ongoing educational process. The first step in planning a retreat is to identify its goals. Objectives are based on consciously created opportunities to ensure development and education of board members and to solicit the board's feedback on performance matters. [57] Consultation with the board prior to the retreat encourages program input. As the agenda is developed, discussion time is allotted. This opens the floor to pertinent discussion topics that are too brief to be allocated an official time slot or for issues that materialize during the course of the session. If outside facilitators or speakers are used, prescreening is necessary to ensure presentation effectiveness. [58]

Participation in retreats and training sessions takes time. This demonstrates an investment in the organization by the volunteer. Therefore, whether arranging the annual retreat or scheduling training sessions, care must be taken not to "overbook" volunteers.   [59] A fast track to board burnout is overcommitting volunteer time through redundant or unnecessary sessions and meetings.

Keeping the Motivation Going

Although alluded to, this chapter has not emphasized the importance of immediate board involvement for new members. Job descriptions used when recruiting candidates serve as springboards. Recruits agree to serve because they believe they can make a difference, that their skills and experience are needed, and that they possess the credentials to accomplish the tasks identified in the job description. It is critical, then, that members begin working on assigned tasks. The volunteer president, paid executive director, and/or appropriate staff members furnish resources for tasks to be accomplished successfully. Encouragement by the aforementioned persons or a "board buddy" should be offered.

It is not advisable, however, to delegate a major task to a new board member. Assignments should be helpful to the organization and leave the new member with a positive feeling. Writing letters to potential donors, using connections in the fund-raising process,   [60] attending special programs to demonstrate board support, and serving as a co-chair on a committee activity quickly involve new members.

The volunteer chair or president must demonstrate a willingness to commit time and invest personal resources into the nonprofit as well. Example by leadership is often the best means by which to establish requirements and define the high standards expected of new members.

The executive director and staff identify and utilize motivational techniques. One such method is to conduct status checks on board and committee work. A telephone call may suffice. Yet taking the time to ask how work is progressing or if the staff needs to lend a helping hand apprises the volunteer of two important facts. First, the progress of work is monitored. Therefore, duty cannot be ignored. Second, staff is ready, willing, and able to support volunteer effort. If more resources are required for a project, the volunteer knows assistance is available.

An extension of this technique is for the executive director to initiate discussion with board members regarding deadlines for specifically assigned tasks. During this discussion, the job description is convenient. This "check-up" approach applies to every aspect of board member performance, from recruiting volunteers for special events to rewriting bylaws to raising funds. On a large task, positive feedback for the accomplishment of various steps makes the volunteer feel appreciated.

Recognition for continued success is important, too. Receiving timely recognition allows board members to experience the feeling of accomplishment for each effort.

Typically, the public relations team is entrenched in the process. What types of recognition can the PR professional provide? A public "thank you" can appear in the nonprofit's newsletter in the form of a mention in a donor list, a feature article, or the executive director's letter. Since the newsletter is sent to a distribution list, the volunteer knows that everyone affiliated with the nonprofit is aware of his or her effort. If a newsletter is forwarded to the volunteer's supervisor at work or to family members, additional recognition value is added.

When the "success story" merits, the PR staff shares the news with a larger audience by sending a news release to appropriate media. For example, notification of new board of directors' members and officers, results of the fund-raising chair's successful campaign efforts, or the names of individuals who received special awards at the nonprofit's annual meeting are excellent content for brief news releases. Such media attention provides public recognition for the volunteer and keeps the nonprofit in the news, drawing positive attention.

The public relations pro must look for tasteful opportunities to integrate volunteer recognition with business. The annual meeting is a public event where appreciation for special service is shown. Members rotating off of the board are thanked for their years of service with a plaque, certificate, or other gift. Officer roles and chair posts being accepted for the upcoming year can be announced as well. Victory celebrations provide another outlet for volunteer recognition. Publicly thanking individuals during a speech or presenting awards for significant contributions make board members feel rewarded for their efforts.

Of course, a kickoff event to any major campaign or program offers advance recognition and helps to build interest and momentum for an effort. Kickoffs provide immediate recognition of those who accepted the challenge, increasing enthusiasm and acting as an incentive for leaders who "have their reputations on the line" to be successful.

Board members can be thanked in other, less-flamboyant ways, such as an acknowledgment at a board meeting. [61] Also, the importance of thank-you notes can never be overrated. Even if worded and mailed by the public relations professional, this personal note provides immediate acknowledgment, especially when signed by the executive director or president.

Making a board member feel like an insider is an inexpensive and easy way to strengthen the bond between the volunteer and the nonprofit. This is achieved by soliciting input, brainstorming over a cup of coffee or lunch, or asking various staff members to update the member (in his or her area of responsibility) prior to announcements at a board meeting. Such tactics encourage a sense of belonging and teamwork.

Whether at the annual meeting or a victory celebration, recognition can include a token of appreciation. "Always give them a small memento to remind them of your organization and appreciation," advises P. Burke Keegan. [62] Pins, plaques, and scrolls are inexpensive, yet they are often proudly displayed by volunteers. In fact, Brian O'Connell, founding president of the Independent Sector, suggests that those volunteers who have made tremendous contributions deserve recognition costing more than a few pennies:

> It appalls me that organizations that receive thousands, if not hundreds of thousands, of dollars of free time balk at spending more than five dollars for a recognition gift. I'm with volunteers a great deal in their offices and homes and know how much these mementos mean. Despite the warped frames, curled paper, or amateurish calligraphy, the awards remain proudly displayed. [63]

A duty frequently assigned to the public relations practitioner is the ordering of mementos and gifts. It is in the best interest of the nonprofit to tastefully display the name of the organization and/or its logo on the award. While the recipient of the award receives recognition by displaying the item, the organization benefits with "free advertising." [64]

When volunteers feel uninvolved or unappreciated, retention of board members and their ongoing support becomes a problem. However, as with anything, recognition can be "overdone." If recognition is diluted by frequency or insignificance, an unjustified expectation materializes, placing little value on the acknowledgment. To secure the proper amount of commendation without overreacting, the public relations practitioner can test the recognition factor in three ways: form, reason, and source.

"Form" refers to the format used. Will recognition be at a high level and in public, such as when a special award is presented at an annual meeting? Or will the acknowledgment be a personal thank-you note or words of praise at a board meeting?

"Reason" refers to why the board member is recognized. Did the volunteer chair a successful fund-raising event or lead the annual fund drive? Or has the volunteer served as a director for the maximum number of terms, even held office, and is now rotating off the board?

"Source" refers to where the acknowledgment originates. Is the national or parent organization acknowledging the individual's efforts? Or have the executive director and other board members determined that recognition should be awarded? [65]

All three factors are considered in a combined equation to determine the most appropriate way to recognize board members.

Evaluation

Ongoing training and recognition help maintain a high level of board commitment. Ongoing support and enthusiasm keep a board of directors vibrant, too. However, even with this, some directors are "dead wood" before their terms expire. Board job descriptions and individual volunteer records ensure an accurate and honest appraisal of members.

As previously mentioned, a volunteer file is established on each board member. This database contains the material collected when the individual initially joined the board. It is updated with committees chaired, offices held, and special assignments completed. Appropriate information is pulled from these files to assist the volunteer in conducting a self-evaluation. In fact, it is helpful to have a form for members to complete after their first year on the board.   (See Form 5.5.) This approach helps new directors see the progress they've made during their brief tenure or realize their level of commitment. This self-assessment, along with peer reviews, group appraisals, and/or board evaluations, can be conducted annually.   [66]

SUCCESSION PLANNING

A nonprofit must establish continuity in leadership, vision, partnerships, and supporters to retain its base and grow. The only way to experience success is to develop and maintain a strong board. Carefully orchestrated succession plans guarantee that quality directors remain in place or are added to the board. The process of selecting, recruiting, training, motivating, retaining, and ultimately rotating board of director personnel should be thought of as an ongoing succession-planning process.

Of course, the first step is a board review. After that, a determination is made as to what changes or status quo arrangements are necessary. These decisions are imperative to ensure the optimum blend of personalities and talents on the board. For those who demonstrate outstanding leadership skills or exhibit key strengths, a career development plan may be confidentially initiated. This strategic approach promotes individual growth, while it adheres to a leadership plan that maximizes the nonprofit's effectiveness. Likewise, weak links on the board are replaced eventually.

When board members retire, the most appropriate replacement is selected. For example, is medical knowledge needed because a doctor is rotating off the board? Perhaps a lawyer is stepping down, and someone with legal insight is needed. Or does someone of a particular gender or person of color need to be asked? Matching the individual qualities and talents of the potential board member to those of the person leaving creates a strategically developed board—one that reflects the "perfect mix." Once such a board is established, this delicate balance must be maintained.

FORM 5.5. New Member Self-Assessment Form

Please complete the following form. It will assist you in evaluating the progress you've made during your first year serving on the board of directors. After you complete this form, please return it to (name) in the (name of nonprofit) office, located at (address).

If after you complete this worksheet, you want additional training to help you grow as a board member, please let us know. We will do our best to make your experience of serving on our board of directors a rewarding one.

Name: _____ Date: _____

In response to the following questions, please write "1" in front of those tasks completed during your first year serving on the board. Please write "2" in front of those items you hope to accomplish during the upcoming year.

1. Understand (name of nonprofit)'s mission and objectives:

_____ Read my board manual
_____ Read print material about the organization
_____ Am familiar with basic responsibilities of board membership
_____ Completed new board member orientation

2. Support the executive director:

_____ Took time to personally meet with the executive director
_____ Discussed with the executive director and volunteer president special
       ways I could serve the nonprofit
_____ Served as a committee chair

3. I believe I have an understanding of:

_____ The organization's legal responsibilities
_____ Community needs and resources
_____ Terminology used by the organization
_____ The staff's roles and the effective staff-committee relationship
_____ The nonprofit's program offerings and services
_____ The organization's long-range vision and plan
_____ Pertinent fiscal details

4. Monitor programs and services:

_____ Observed services provided by (name of nonprofit)
_____ Attended special events or programs

FORM 5.5 (*continued*)

5. Help to ensure the nonprofit has adequate resources:

____ Pledged and made payment(s) to the capital campaign and/or annual fund drive

____ Made solicitation visits or cultivation calls requested by the development staff

Names of individuals, corporations, or foundations called upon:

_____

_____

_____

_____

_____

____ I have telephoned or written notes on invitations to special events or annual fund drive mailings to the following individuals:

_____

_____

_____

_____

_____

____ When appropriate, I have introduced colleagues and friends to the nonprofit and its mission and goals

____ I have supplied names and addresses of the following individuals to be added to (name of nonprofit)'s mailing list:

_____

_____

_____

6. Enhance the organization's public image:

____ Taken an active role in the speakers bureau

____ Worn and displayed objects with the nonprofit's logo

____ Taken advantage of opportunities to share information about (name of nonprofit) with government officials, community leaders, media representatives, and friends

7. New ideas:

____ Made the following suggestions to the executive director, board members, or chairs:

_____

_____

_____

____ If approved or agreed upon, I helped develop and execute the following recommendations:

_____

_____

_____

8. **Please answer the following questions in regard to the time commitment spent during the past year:**

   A. **On average, how many hours do you donate through your participation on the board and committees and by attending events?**
- ____ 1 to 5 hours per month
- ____ 6 to 15 hours per month
- ____ 16 to 25 hours per month
- ____ More than 25 hours per month

   B. **Meeting participation:**
- ____ Regularly attended board of director meetings
- ____ Regularly attended committee meetings
- ____ Served on at least one committee
- ____ If unable to attend a committee or board meeting, I notify the appropriate person
- ____ Read agendas, minutes, reports, and other pertinent material prior to meetings
- ____ Attend conferences, workshops, seminars, or ongoing training opportunities

9. **The following reference materials would be helpful to me:** _____

_____

_____

_____

10. **It would be advantageous to hear experts discuss or have workshops held on the following topics:** _____

_____

_____

_____

Making the Grade

Whether reviewing the credentials of existing board members or potential volunteers, the following criteria should be used to measure each individual:

- Can this person assist the development, interpretation, and execution of policy?
- Can this individual critically evaluate the organization and take the appropriate action?
- Is this person able to hire and, if necessary, fire the executive director?

- Will this person be an excellent representative of the organization in the community?
- Will this individual give and raise money for the nonprofit? [67]
- Will this person actively maintain the organization's legal and ethical integrity and accountability?
- Is this individual capable of overseeing the management of the group's resources?
- Will this person recruit and orient new board members as well as honestly assess board performance? [68]
- Does this person bring a talent or skill to the board that is needed by the organization?
- Will this person add diversity to the director group, helping the nonprofit to reflect the community or population it represents?
- Does this individual have a conflict of interest that would prohibit the person from serving the nonprofit?

The criteria for selecting a board member is stringent, but the aforementioned areas are crucial to a board of directors' performance.

A Final Comment

A formal recruiting strategy permits the board to evolve in a direction that enables the nonprofit to move toward its long-term vision. This strategy not only sets the stage for board quality but does so in a timely manner while developing an extensive network of committed contacts.

Glossary

against the grain —Folding paper at right angles to the grain of the paper.

alignment —Refers to the placement of type in a column or on a full page. Type can be centered. If type is flush left or flush right, it means that type is evenly aligned to the left or to the right with the other side appearing ragged. Justified type appears without any ragged edges at the end of lines.

annual report —An organizational publication that records accomplishments of interest to stockholders and is issued on an annual basis. Publicly traded companies must comply with Securities and Exchange standards, which require detailed financial data to be included in this document. Entities not required by law to produce this type of report frequently do so for public relations purposes.

art—Any pictorial matter such as photos, illustrations, cartoons, charts, or graphs.

articulation —The ability to correctly form the sound of a word. Poor articulation results when sounds or syllables are omitted, another sound is substituted for the correct one, or when sounds are added where they do not belong.

audience —The receivers of a message. The term may apply to readers of publications, such as a newsletter or an annual report. "Audience" is also used in public speaking to refer to a group gathered to hear a speaker or see a presentation.

bandwagon —Social phenomenon in which an increasing number of people are motivated to adopt a philosophy or try an activity, as can be the case with crowd behavior.

bar graph —Art displaying statistics through the use of bars in various lengths.

bars—Thick lines, usually placed horizontally to separate text and/or visuals.

benchmark study —An initial measurement of audience attitude and opinions before a public relations campaign is initiated. Attitude is measured later to determine what change, if any, occurred as a result of the campaign.

bleed—A photograph or graphic element that appears to extend off the page.

blueline—A printing term for the position proof of a document developed from the final film that will be used to make printing plates. Created through a photographic process, the exact dimension, type, imagery, etc. of the final piece is produced in a blue shade. The blueline is used as a final proof prior to the press run.

body copy—Text written in relatively small point size and set in a "block" form.

boldface—Heavy, black type.

border—A line or art designed to surround copy or art. This treatment establishes definite edges for the material.

bulk mailing—A term used to refer to the U.S. Postal Service third-class mail. Parcels must be presorted and bundled by zip code in order to receive a special low-cost mailing rate.

busy—A design term used to describe a visual with too many elements for the amount of space. Consequently, elements compete with each other.

byline—A line citing the author of an article. The credit line may be placed at the beginning or the end of the article.

camera-ready—Material that needs no further treatment and is suitable for photographing in the offset printing process or duplicating copy.

clip art—A previously created line art or graphic design available in print form or on a diskette. This material can be used for a wide variety of purposes such as in a newsletter, brochure, or on slides. Rights are purchased to use this art, or it may be available from the public domain.

color separation—Full-color art is broken into the four primary color components of magenta, cyan, yellow, and black.

column—A regular feature or article in a publication. In the layout process, the term refers to the text that runs from the top to the bottom of a page.

communications apprehension—Anxiety produced when an individual faces a public speaking setting. This apprehension is usually categorized into four types: trait-like, situational, audience-based, and context-based.

communications audit —Use of research techniques and methodology for an organization to systematically review and analyze how well it communicates to its target publics.

community relations —The field of public relations that deals with building relationships with the various publics, such as neighborhoods, schools, and churches, with which an organization conducts business or in which it is based.

condensed type —A typeface that retains design integrity, but that has narrower characters.

copyright—Prohibits others from using the musical, artistic, or literary work of the creator or owner of the material without permission.

contrast—The range of black to white tones in a scanned photograph. A high-contrast photo shows an extensive range from full black to full white. A low-contrast photo has "light" blacks and "gray" whites.

copy fitting —Writing copy to fit the amount of space available.

copy testing —Submitting copy to a small group of people to receive a response. This effort helps to determine what set of words or message will be the most effective before distributing to the entire audience.

crop—Eliminating unnecessary or undesired portions of a photograph or art. Cropping also occurs when the photograph or art is altered to change proportions.

cutlines—The brief statement identifying a photograph.

decoder—Receiver of a message.

demographics —Identifying characteristics of the public, such as age or education, used to categorize a population.

desktop publishing —Use of a personal computer and software to format camera-ready material for printing. Material can be transferred by diskette or modem to a printer. Output can also be in the form of a laser print.

display type —Type used for headlines or to emphasize various elements in the layout. This type is larger than 12 points.

drop shadow —An effect created by placing a shadow, typically behind a boxed area. This graphic technique creates a three-dimensional look.

dummy —A preliminary layout including positions of illustrations and text as they will appear in the final production. Also refers to the blank pages made up to show what the size, shape, form, and basic style of the printed piece will be like.

duotone —A halftone reproduction of a black and white photograph done in two colors.

embossing —A finishing operation in the printing process that produces a relief image, accomplished by pressing paper between special dies.

ethos—In the public speaking environment, this refers to a speaker's credibility.

feedback—The response the receiver of a message gives to the sender, which indicates how the message was interpreted.

flow chart —A diagram that depicts a step-by-step process of an activity.

font—The type characters of a specific typeface and size. This includes the full alphabet and number and symbol sets.

formatting —Establishing the guidelines for page layout or word-processing programs. This includes factors such as spacing, indentation, line length, and justification.

four-color process —The printing process that uses magenta, yellow, cyan, and black to produce full color; also called "process color."

freelancer —A writer, artist, photographer, or designer who works independently and is called in by an organization to perform an occasional job.

gatefold—A cover that opens out, producing two additional pages. Annual reports sometimes have a gatefold.

glossy print —A picture with a glossy, smooth surface. This type of photograph reproduces better in the printing process than a picture with a matte finish.

grain—In the printing process, the direction in which the majority of the fibers lie. This determines the direction in which paper is easiest to fold.

grid—A matrix comprised of vertical and horizontal lines that guides the layout process. A grid is not used for the actual printing of a piece but for the placement of text and graphics on the page.

grouped line chart —Multiple lines positioned on a single grid. To differentiate between the multiple lines, contrasting patterns, line widths, or colors are used.

gutter—The vertical space that appears between columns.

halftone—In the printing process, a continuous-tone is broken into a high-contrast pattern of small dots, so they can be reproduced on the printing press.

headline—Large type used to grab attention in an ad or to call attention to the title of a story or news article.

illustration —A drawing, painting, or sketch.

jumpline—The term used when an article must be continued on a subsequent page or is a continuation from a previous location. A phrase, such as "continued on the next page" or "continued from page 5," is included.

landscape —Horizontal orientation of a page.

layout—The arrangement of the elements of a printed piece into a defined space in a manner that is pleasing to look at as well as readable.

lc—In typography, a word printed in lowercase letters.

logo—A stylized graphic or lettering used to denote a particular product or service. Typically, an organization's logo is trade-marked, so its identity remains unique.

logos—In a public speaking context, the rhetorical appeal to logic.

masthead —Found in a newsletter or newspaper, this block of information lists the publisher's name and address, subscription details, and staff names.

mean—The arithmetic average of scores.

median—The midpoint in a series of scores; the point above and below which 50 percent of the values in a series of numbers are recorded.

medium—Any single media, such as a newspaper, a magazine, or a television station.

mode—The most frequently occurring value in a series of numbers.

moiré pattern —An undesirable pattern that destroys detail and creates uneven tonal values. This effect is produced when a screened halftone is screened again.

multiple bar chart —A basic bar graph serves at the foundation of this graphic device, but the quantitative value of two or more sets of variables are displayed within the same exhibit.

nameplate —The title of the newsletter or newspaper as it appears on the front page of the publication. Typically, special type size and style are used to create a distinctive appearance for this title.

newsletter —A publication containing information for a target audience. Newsletters are issued on a routine basis and have a variety of purposes. This printed piece can disclose news about the organization producing the newsletter or be commercially published on select topics and supported by subscribers.

nonprofit —An organization engaged in activities not intended to produce a profit. Instead, the entity focuses on public rather than private gain. To possess this tax-exempt status, the organization must qualify by filing for this privilege with the Internal Revenue Service as well as by meeting specific IRS criteria.

offset printing —A common printing method in which film negatives are used to make printing plates. Camera-ready materials are required for this printing process.

orphan —A word or single line of a paragraph that appears by itself on the top of a page or column.

overrun —When more than the number of specified copies is printed.

paste-up —All type and graphic material are combined into a single layout for reproduction.

pathos —In rhetorical terms, an emotional appeal.

perfect binding —Pages and cover are held together with an adhesive. After the cover is glued to the spine of the book, the cover and pages are trimmed as a unit.

photo permission form —A written agreement granting permission to use a person's photograph in a publication such as a newsletter or annual report. To be legal, this document must be signed by the photographed subject or a legal guardian or parent. Also referred to as a model or a talent release. Frequently, at least $1 is paid for the photo appearance.

pica—A horizontal unit of measurement used by printers. Six picas are equal to 1 inch.

pictogram—A highly simplified visual representation of objects or qualities used to depict a story or meaning, such as to communicate statistical data.

pie chart—A visual that subdivides a pie-shaped graph into individual components to depict what comprises the whole. Each component is a wedge of the circle. Typically the largest value is drawn as the first slice of the circle, and it begins at the 12 o'clock position.

pitch—In public speaking, the height of one's voice; how high or how low the vocal sound is.

PMS—Abbreviation for Pantone Matching System, a proprietary ink color mixing system.

point—The unit of measurement referring to the height of type. Twelve points equal 1 pica.

politically correct—Trying not to offend an individual or group of persons by refraining from using statements or actions that demean or stereotype on the basis of religion, ethnic background, sex, religion, race, sexual orientation, physical characteristics, or personal beliefs.

process color—*See* four-color process.

pronunciation—The ability of a speaker to say each word correctly. This includes the proper sound and the proper accent.

public relations—A planned and deliberate process that includes research and analysis in order to identify, establish, and maintain relationships that are mutually beneficial between an organization and its constituent publics.

pull quotes—In a newsletter, newspaper, or magazine article, quotations pulled from the text, printed in a larger point size, and set off from the copy in a manner that draws a reader's attention to the extracted material.

psychographics—Helps to define the qualitative differences among people. This measures criteria such as lifestyles, personal goals, values, and psychological traits.

RACE—An acronym used in the public relations discipline and developed by John Marston. The "R" stands for "research"; the

"A" stands for "action and planning"; the "C" stands for "communication"; and the "E" stands for "evaluation."

ragged—One side of a column of type is left uneven or unjustified.

rate—In a public speaking situation, the speed with which a speech is delivered. Most professional speakers average between 120 to 180 words per minute.

resolution—The degree of definition and clarity provided by an output device. A laser printer is an example of an output device. Included in a printer's specs is its resolution capability.

reverse—Graphics and text are "reversed" from the usual appearance by having white (or light) print appear against black or a dark background.

saddle stitch—A commonly used method to bind a document. The booklet is opened and wires are inserted through the backbone. The remaining three sides are then trimmed.

sans serif—In typography, no cross strokes or "flags" appear at the top or bottom of a letter.

scaling—When printing, an element may be enlarged or reduced from its original size. Therefore, it is "scaled" to the desired size.

screen—A shaded appearance used as background for text or graphics. A solid color appears at 100 percent of screen; whereas, white is at 0 percent. A screen occurs when the color is not printed at a 100 percent screen. Screens can be dark, such as producing the color at 90 percent, or very light, such as printing at 10 percent. The term "screen" also refers to the dot pattern used in the process of creating a halftone from a photograph.

script—In printing, a typeface that looks like handwriting.

score—To impress or indent the location in the paper where a fold is to occur to make the folding easier. Typically, cover stock or paper that will be folded against the grain is scored.

SEC—Securities and Exchange Commission.

serif—The "flags" or cross strokes that appear on the bottom and top of letters within certain typefaces. These typefaces are referred to as "serif typefaces."

sidebar—A brief written piece that supplements a lengthy article by offering extra detail or insight. Because the focus is on the same subject as the longer piece, the sidebar is positioned nearby in the layout.

slide—Photographic film, usually mounted in a paper frame but sometimes housed in a metal frame. The film is shown on a screen by a slide projection unit.

software—Computer programs that contain information enabling the hardware to perform specialized operations such as spreadsheets or word processing.

spatial organizational pattern —An outline that organizes items or thought according to direction or location in order to guide the development of a speech.

speakers bureau —A group of individuals trained to represent an organization and to deliver speeches on particular subject matter to civic clubs, schools, special interest groups, or any target audiences identified as being critical to the organization's public relations strategy.

spiral binding —Holes are drilled or punched through the publication after it is printed and collated. Wire or plastic is inserted into the holes and serves as a binder for the document.

spot color—A primary color, such as black, is used in the printing process, and the art is strategically accented with a second color. A specific ink color is used as the second color rather than one that is "built" through process color.

spread—The two pages that face each other in a layout.

stockholder —An investor or shareholder in a business.

strategy—The public relations approach to problem solving in which various components, such as target audience and message, are identified and analyzed and a plan of action is devised to address the specific situation.

subhead—A brief heading placed inside long bodies of copy to break up a long block of text. The term also applies to a display line that expands on the primary headline.

surface chart —A line chart serves as the foundation of this type of chart. The effect is produced by creating colored or shaded areas of surface between the trend and base lines.

tactics—Specific techniques utilized to accomplish strategic goals. These methods, developed in a progressive order, describe how to achieve PR objectives.

target audience —Also known as "target publics," the constituency identified as being the primary recipient of the communication or PR effort.

temporal organizational pattern —The content of a speech arranged in sequential order.

theme—A statement or phrase designed for repetition and to stand as the primary message an organization wants to communicate to its publics. The theme can also be carried through graphic devices, by word of mouth, or in written form.

thumbnail —A rough, miniature layout.

tone—The attitude or feeling of a message.

topical organizational pattern —A popular outline used for the development of an informative speech. Subject matter is conveniently divided into equally important subpoints for discussion purposes.

trademark—A device, name, or symbol registered for the exclusive use of its owner or creator to identify a product.

typography —The field that refers to the designing, setting, and using of type.

uc—In typography, this refers to printing letters in uppercase or capitals.

vocal segregate —An intruding phrase or sound originating from a speaker. Vocal segregates can distract the audience by interrupting the flow of the speaker's presentation.

white space —The blank space in a layout or design where no text, photos, or graphics appear. White space is considered a design element.

widow—A letter or single line of a paragraph appearing at the bottom of a page or column.

World Wide Web —The portion of the Internet that delivers information and entertainment through the use of color, printed words, sound, and illustrations.

wraparound —Lines of type that vary in length to wrap or flow around an illustration, silhouetted photo, or other graphic device.

Notes

Chapter 1

1. Bruce R. Hopkins, "The Legal Context of Nonprofit Enterprise,*The Nonprofit Entrepreneur: Creating Ventures to Earn Income*(New York: The Foundation Center, 1988), pp. 11-12.

2. Thomas Wolf,*Managing a Nonprofit Organization*(New York: Simon and Schuster, 1990), pp. 5-8.

3. Hopkins, pp. 12-13.

4. Virginia A. Hodgkinson.*Nonprofit Almanac, 1996-1997*(San Francisco: Jossey-Bass, Inc., 1996), p. 49.

5. Lester M. Salamon and Helmut K. Anheier*The Emerging Nonprofit Sector: An Overview*, Johns Hopkins Nonprofit Sector Series 1(New York: Manchester University Press, 1996), p. xvii.

6. *Giving and Volunteering in the United States: Findings from a National Survey.* 1996 Edition(Washington, DC: Independent Sector, 1996, pp. 3-83.

7. *Giving and Volunteering in the United States*,pp. 3-78.

8. Rayna Skolnik, "Rebuilding Trust: Nonprofits Act to Boost Reputations," *Public Relations Journal,*September 1993, p. 31.

9. Rayna Skolnik, "Rebuilding Trust: Nonprofits Act to Boost Reputations," *Public Relations Journal,*September 1993, p. 29.

10. Scott M. Cutlip,*Fundraising in the United States: Its Role in America's Philanthropy* (New Brunswick, NJ: Transaction Publishers, 1990) pp. 206-207.

11. *America's Nonprofit Sector in Brief*(Washington, DC: Independent Sector, 1998), p. 2.

12. Ann E. Kaplan, ed.,*Giving USA 1999*(New York: American Association of Fundraising Counsel, 1999, p. 43.

13. *America's Nonprofit Sector in Brief*p. 2.

14. Kaplan, p. 12.

15. Kaplan, p. 28.

16. Kaplan, p. 22.

17. Salamon and Anheier, p. xviii.

18. Philip Kotler and Alan Andreasen,*Strategic Marketing for Nonprofit Organizations*, Fourth Edition(Englewood Cliffs, NJ: Prentice-Hall, Inc., 1991, p. 568.

19. James T. Bennett, "Assessing Charitable Organizations,"*Consumer's Research.*

20. *Riley v. National Federation of the Blind of North Carolina, Inc*87-328-487 U.S. 781, 1085 CT 2867, L101, Ed., p. 669(March 23, 1988) (June 29, 1988).

21. James T. Bennett, "Assessing Charitable Organizations,"*Consumer's Research,* May 1991, p. 16.

22. Bennett, p. 17.

23. Marc J. Epstein, "The Fall of Corporate Charitable Contributions,*Public Relations Quarterly,* Summer 1993, p. 37.

24. Dennis L. Wilcox, Phillip H. Ault, and Warren K. Agee,*Public Relations: Strategies and Tactics,* Fourth Edition (New York: HarperCollins College Publishers, 1995), p. 6.

25. Wilcox, Ault, and Agee, p. 9.

26. Todd Hunt and James E. Grunig,*Public Relations Techniques*(New York: Harcourt Brace Publishers, 1994), p. 9.

27. Kotler and Andreasen, p. 570.

28. Wilcox, Ault, and Agee, p. 17.

29. Robert Kendall,*Public Relations Campaign Strategies: Planning for Implementation,* Second Edition (New York: HarperCollins College Publishers, 1996) p. 5.

30. Wilcox, Ault, and Agee, p. 15.

31. Kendall, p. 5.

32. David L. Rados,*Marketing for Nonprofit Organizations,* Second Edition (Westport, CT: Auburn House, 1996), p. 282.

33. *Promoting Issues and Ideas: A Guide to Public Relations for Nonprofit Organizations*(New York: The Foundation Center, 1987), pp. 1-2.

34. Rados, p. 355.

35. Kotler and Andreasen, p. 573.

Chapter 2

1. *The 1997 Potlatch Annual Report Show: The Essentials*(Cloquet, MN: Potlatch Corporation, 1997), p. 68.

2. Denis Connors, "A Fertile Annual Report Market,"*Public Relations Quarterly,* Winter 1991-1992, p. 34.

3. Allan B. Afterman and Rowan H. Jones,*Nonprofit Accounting and Auditing Disclosure Manual 1993*(Boston, MA: Warren Gorham Lamont, 1993), pp. 1-2.

4. Milton Murray and Ken Turpen, "Annual Reports that Raise Money,*Fund Raising Management,* June 1996, p. 48.

5. Glenn Hasek, "Adding Art to Numbers,"*Industry Week,* November 17 1997, pp. 122-124.

6. *Investor Relations Surveys: Annual Report*(Vienna, VA: National Investor Relations Institute, 1996), p. 5.

7. *Investor Relations Surveys,* p. 5.

8. *The 1997 Potlatch Annual Report Show,*p. 69.

9. *Investor Relations Surveys,* p. 6.

10. Hasek, p. 122.

11. *Investor Relations Surveys,* p. 7.

12. *Guidelines for Publishing a Minimum Annual Report*(Washington, DC: Council on Foundations, 1983), p. 2.

13. Hasek, p. 125.

14. *Investor Relations Survey,* p. 6.

15. *Guidelines for Publishing a Minimum Annual Report,* p. 2.

16. *Investor Relations Survey,* p. 6.

17. *A Study of Corporate Annual Reports* (Cloquet, MN: Potlatch Corporation, 1995), p. 11.

18. Gene Zelazny, *Say It with Charts,* Third Edition (Chicago: Irwin Professional Publishing, 1996), pp. 38-40.

19. Zelazny, p. 33.

20. Zelazny, p. 28.

21. *Investor Relations Survey,* p. 6.

22. *Investor Relations Survey,* p. 7.

23. *Investor Relations Survey,* p. 6.

24. Dennis L. Wilcox and Lawrence W. Nolte, *Public Relations: Writing and Media Techniques,* Second Edition (New York: HarperCollins College Publishers, 1995), p. 312.

25. Bivens, Thomas, *Handbook for Public Relations Writing,* Third Edition (Lincolnwood, IL: NTC Business Books, 1995), pp. 176-177.

26. *The A.R. Client* (Cloquet, MN: Potlach Corporation, 1996), p. 10.

27. *The 1997 Potlatch Annual Report Show,* p. 69.

28. Nanette Wright, *Blueline Guideline* (New York: Wright Communications, 1998), p. 7.

29. "Survey: Annual Reports Repurposed from Print to Web Are on Rise," *Graphic Design,* June 1997, p. 22.

30. Pamela Moore, "CD Won't Go Platinum, but Heck, It's an Annual Report," *The Charlotte Observer,* March 18, 1996, p. 3D.

31. *Investor Relations Survey,* p. 8.

32. Hasek, p. 127.

Chapter 3

1. Theodore E. Conover, *Graphic Communications Today,* Second Edition (New York: West Publishing Company, 1990) pp. 204-205.

2. Dennis L. Wilcox and Lawrence W. Nolte, *Public Relations: Writing and Media Techniques,* Second Edition (New York: HarperCollins College Publishers, 1995), p. 351.

3. Howard Penn Hudson, *Publishing Newsletters,* Revised Edition (New York: Charles Scribner's Sons, 1988), pp. 1-2.

4. Hudson, pp. 6-8.

5. Thomas Bivens, *Fundamentals of Successful Newsletters* (Lincolnwood, IL: NTC Business Books, 1993), pp. 10-11.

6. Todd Hunt and James Grunig, *Public Relations Techniques* (New York: Harcourt Brace Publishers, 1994), p. 14.

7. Bivens, *Fundamentals of Successful Newsletters,* p. 12.

8. Barbara A. Fanson, *Producing a First-Class Newsletter* (Bellingham, WA: Self-Counsel Press, 1994), p. 7.

9. Roger C. Parker, *Newsletters from the Desktop* (Chapel Hill, NC: Ventana Press, 1990), p. 6.

10. Elaine Floyd, *Marketing with Newsletters* Second Edition (St. Louis, MO: Newsletter Resources, 1997, p. 204.

11. Parker, p. 26.

12. Parker, p. 28.

13. Colin Wheildon, *Type & Layout* (Berkeley, CA: Strathmoor Press, 1995, p. 125.

14. Floyd, p. 202.

15. Wilcox and Nolte, p. 349.

16. Parker, p. 29.

17. Floyd, p. 202.

18. Floyd, p. 202.

19. Parker, p. 32.

20. Parker, p. 35.

21. Parker, p. 36.

22. Parker, p. 62.

23. Fanson, pp. 56-57.

24. Floyd, p. 198.

25. Parker, p. 87.

26. Floyd, p. 198.

27. Floyd, p. 200.

28. Wheildon, p. 110.

29. Bivens, *Fundamentals of Successful Newsletters*, p. 67.

30. Bivens, *Fundamentals of Successful Newsletters*, p. 83.

31. Bivens, *Fundamentals of Successful Newsletters*, p. 84.

32. Philip N. Douglis, "Natural Response Key to Informal Portraits," *IABC Communication World* November 1991, p. 42.

33. Dustin Peck, KPC Photography, Charlotte, NC. Personal interview. June 27, 1998.

34. Philip N. Douglis, "How Eyes Can Express Meaning in Pictures," *IABC Communication World* April-May 1997, p. 41.

35. Peck, June 27, 1998.

36. Philip N. Douglis, "Get Up, Get Down for Better Portraits," *IABC Communication World* January 1991, p. 40.

37. Philip N. Douglis, "Good Photographers Climb High, Shoot Down," *IABC Communication World* December 1993, p. 42.

38. Philip N. Douglis, "Cover Meetings with Varied Viewpoints," *IABC Communication World* September 1993, p. 49.

39. Philip N. Douglis, "When Sequence and Placement Make the Point," *IABC Communication World* August 1992, p. 31.

40. Peck, June 27, 1998.

41. Conover, p. 111.

42. Larry Raymond,*Reinventing Communication: A Guide to Using Visual Language for Planning, Problem Solving, and Reengineering*(Milwaukee, WI: ASQC Quality Press, 1994), p. 60.

43. Patricia A. Williams,*Creating and Producing the Perfect Newsletter*(Glenview, IL: Scott, Foresman, and Company, 1991) p. 210.

44. Peggy Nelson,*How to Create Powerful Newsletters*(Chicago, IL: Bonus Books, Inc., 1993), p. 4.

45. Conover, pp. 137-138.

46. Margie Storch, Storch Design, Charlotte, NC. Personal interview, June 25, 1998.

47. Barbara Radke Blake and Barbara L. Stein,*Creating Newsletters, Brochures, and Pamphlets*(New York: Neal-Schuman Publishers, Inc., 1992, p. 14.

48. Bivens,*Fundamentals of Successful Newsletters*,p. 17.

49. Wes Westmoreland, Westmoreland Printers, Inc. Shelby, NC. Personal interview. June 24, 1998.

50. *How to Plan Printing*(Boston, MA: S.D. Warren Company, 1988) pp. 76-77.

51. Conover, p. 148.

52. James Craig, *Production for the Graphic Designer*(New York: Watson-Guptill Publications, 1974), p. 178.

53. *How to Plan Printing* pp. 77-78.

54. Floyd, pp. 218-219.

55. Floyd, p. 221.

56. Wheildon, p. 122.

57. Floyd, p. 221.

58. Wheildon, pp. 124-125.

59. Conover, p. 167.

60. Wilcox and Nolte, p. 348.

61. William Thompson,*Targeting the Message: A Receiver-Centered Process for Public Relations Writing*(White Plains, NY: Longman Publishers, 1996) p. 240.

62. Williams, pp. 69-72.

63. Marvin Arth and Helen Ashmore,*The Newsletter Editor's Desk Book*,Third Edition (Shawnee Mission, KS: Parkway Press, 1984) p. 50.

64. "Good Captions—Good in Content and in Form—Are Potent Typographic Tools for Readership,"*Editor's Workshop,* February 1992, p. 8.

65. Debra Hart May,*Proofreading: Plain and Simple*(Franklin Lakes, NJ: Career Press, 1997), pp. 47-52.

66. May, pp. 118-119.

67. Thomas Bivens,*Handbook for Public Relations Writing*,Third Edition(Lincolnwood, IL: NTC Business Books, 1995, p. 26.

68. Wilcox and Nolte, p. 491.

69. May, pp. 130-131.

70. *How to Conduct a Readership Survey*(New York: Editor's Newsletter, n.d.), p. 3.

71. Dennis L. Wilcox, Phillip H. Ault, and Warren K. Agee,*Public Relations: Strategies and Tactics* Fifth Edition (New York: Addison Wesley Longman, Inc., 1998), p. 204.

72. Mark Beach, *Newsletter Sourcebook* (Cincinnati, OH: F&W Publications, 1993), pp. 3-5.

Chapter 4

1. Lucille A. Maddalena,*A Communications Manual for Nonprofit Organizations* (New York: AMACOM, 1981), p. 55.

2. Terri Horvath,*Spread the Word: How to Promote Nonprofit Groups with a Network of Speakers*(Indianapolis, IN: Publishing resources, 1995) pp. 1-3.

3. *Promoting Issues and Ideas: A Guide to Public Relations for Nonprofit Organizations*(New York: The Foundation Center, 1987, p. 128.

4. Phillip Kotler and Alan Andreasen,*Strategic Marketing for Nonprofit Organizations*, Fourth Edition(Englewood Cliffs, NJ: Prentice Hall, Inc., 1991, p. 587.

5. Bruce E. Gronbeck, Kathleen German, Douglas Ehninger, and Alan Monroe, *Principles of Speech Communication,* Twelfth Edition (New York: HarperCollins College Publishers, 1995, p. 55.

6. Gronbeck et al., p. 56.

7. Sherwyn P. Morreale and Courtland L. Bovee,*Excellence in Public Speaking* (New York: Harcourt Brace College Publishers, 1998 p. 118.

8. Gronbeck et al., p. 58.

9. Morreale and Bovee, p. 119.

10. Steven A. Beebe and Susan J. Beebe,*Public Speaking: An Audience-Centered Approach,* Third Edition(Boston, MA: Allyn & Bacon, 1997, p. 87.

11. Gronbeck et al., p. 59.

12. Gronbeck et al., p. 61.

13. Fraser P. Seitel,*The Practice of Public Relations,*Seventh Edition (Upper Saddle River, NJ: Prentice Hall, 1998, p. 52.

14. Gronbeck et al., p. 245.

15. Beebe and Beebe, pp. 121-124.

16. Devito, Joseph A.*The Elements of Public Speaking,*Fifth Edition (New York: HarperCollins College Publishers, 1994 p. 197.

17. Devito, p. 199.

18. Beebe and Beebe, p. 193.

19. Devito, p. 201.

20. Bill Hill and Charlynn Ross,*Public Speaking: Process and Product,*Second Edition (Dubuque, IA: Kendall Hunt Publishing Company, 1998 pp. 107-108.

21. Devito, p. 202.

22. Hill and Ross, p. 108.

23. Beebe and Beebe, pp. 164-167.

24. Beebe and Beebe, p. 173.

25. Morreale and Bovee, p. 143.

26. Lee W. Huebner, The Value of Effective Speechwriting. In Clarke L. Caywood, ed., *The Handbook of Strategic Public Relations & Integrated Communications* (New York: McGraw-Hill, 1997), p. 534.

27. Devito, p. 413.

28. Dennis L. Wilcox and Lawrence W. Nolte,*Public Relations: Writing and Media Techniques,* Second Edition (New York: HarperCollins College Publishers, 1995), pp. 418-419.

29. Thomas B. Harte, Carolyn Keefe, and Bob R. Derryberry,*The Complete Book of Speechwriting for Students and Professionals,*Third Edition (Edina, MN: Burgess International Group, Inc., 1992, pp. 118-119.

30. Karen Kangas Dwyer,*Conquer Your Speechfright* (New York: Harcourt Brace College Publishers, 1998), p. 10.

31. Dwyer, p. 11.

32. Devito, p. 456.

33. Beebe and Beebe, p. 291.

34. Devito, p. 256.

35. Beebe and Beebe, p. 293.

36. Morreale and Bovee, p. 299.

37. Devito, p. 459.

38. Devito, p. 460.

39. Morreale and Bovee, p. 302.

40. Beebe and Beebe, p. 289.

41. Morreale and Bovee, p. 302.

42. Beebe and Beebe, p. 290.

43. Morreale and Bovee, p. 303.

44. Stephen E. Lucas, *The Art of Public Speaking,* Sixth Edition (Boston: McGraw-Hill, 1998), p. 305.

45. Harte, Keefe, and Derryberry, p. 284.

46. Thomas Bivens, *Handbook for Public Relations Writing,*Third Edition (Chicago, IL: NTC Business Books, 1995, p. 241.

47. Dan Cavanaugh,*Preparing Visual Aids for Presentations* (Boston: Allyn & Bacon, 1997), p. 6.

48. Cavanaugh, p. 12.

49. Larry Raymond, *Reinventing Communication: A Guide to Using Visual Language for Planning, Problem Solving, and Reengineering* (Milwaukee, WI: ASQC Quality Press, 1994), p. 136.

50. Morreale and Bovee, p. 285.

51. Morreale and Bovee, p. 285.

Chapter 5

1. Wayne Clark, "Nonprofits with Strong Boards Will Be Survivors,*The Business Journal,*May 19, 1997, p. 40.

2. Brian O'Connell,*The Board Member's Book,* Second Edition (New York: The Foundation Center, 1993, pp. 21-24.

3. O'Connell,*The Board Member's Book,* p. 25.

4. John Carver, *Boards That Make a Difference* (San Francisco: Jossey-Bass Publishers, 1990), pp. 25-58.

5. Carver, pp. 213-220.

6. *Giving and Volunteering in the United States: Findings from a National Survey,* 1996 Edition (Washington, DC: Independent Sector, 1996) p. 3.

7. *Giving and Volunteering in the United States,* p. I-30.

8. *Giving and Volunteering in the United States,* p. I-54.

9. David L. Rados, *Marketing for Nonprofit Organizations* Second Edition (Westport, CT: Auburn House, 1996) p. 437.

10. *Giving and Volunteering in the United States,* pp. 4-88.

11. O'Connell, *The Board Member's Book* p. 10.

12. Philip Kotler and Alan R. Andreasen, *Strategic Marketing for Nonprofit Organizations* Fifth Edition (Upper Saddle River, NJ: Prentice Hall, 1996) p. 277.

13. Kotler and Andreasen, p. 11.

14. *Giving and Volunteering in the United States,* p. I-35.

15. Rados, p. 445.

16. Douglas C. Eadie, *Boards That Work: A Practical Guide to Building Effective Association Boards* (Washington, DC: American Society of Association Executives, 1994), p. 93.

17. *Serving on the Board of a Tax-Exempt Organization: A Guide for New Directors* (Chicago: Grant Thornton, International, 1993) p. 15.

18. *The Work of a Chapter Board: A Guide for Chapter Board Members* (American Red Cross (Washington, DC, 1995), p. 7.

19. O'Connell, *The Board Member's Book* p. 31.

20. Larry D. Lauer, *Communication Power: Energizing Your Nonprofit Organization* (Gaithersburg, MD: Aspen Publishers, 1997) p. 87.

21. Larry D. Lauer, "How Well Does Your Board Communicate?" *Nonprofit World,* March/April 1997, p. 16.

22. Anthony Mancuso, *How to Form a Nonprofit Corporation* Second Edition (Berkeley, CA: Nolo Press, 1994), p. 28.

23. Kotler and Andreasen, p. 591.

24. *Serving on the Board of a Tax-Exempt Organization,* p. 6.

25. P. Burke Keegan, *Fundraising for Non-Profits* (New York: Times Minnon, 1990), p. 200.

26. Thomas Wolf, *Managing a Nonprofit Organization* (New York: Fireside, 1990), p. 37.

27. Wolf, p. 37.

28. Nancy R. Axelrod, *The Chief Executive's Role in Developing the Nonprofit Board* (New York: National Center for Nonprofit Boards, 1993) pp. 11-16.

29. Brian O'Connell, *Effective Leadership in Voluntary Organizations* (New York: Walker and Company, 1981), p. 150.

30. Carver, p. 143.

31. Lauer, *Communication Power,* pp. 80-81.

32. Maureen K. Robinson, *Developing the Nonprofit Board* (Washington, DC: National Center for Nonprofit Boards, 1994) p. 8.

33. Robert W. Kile and J. Michael Loscavio,*Strategic Board Recruitment: The Not-for-Profit Model*(Gaithersburg, MD: Aspen Publishers, 1996), p. 42.

34. Kile and Loscavio, p. 24.

35. Kim Klein,*Fundraising for Social Change*(Inverness, CA: Chardon Press, 1994), p. 47.

36. Klein, pp. 47-48.

37. Judith Grummon Nelson,*Six Keys to Recruiting, Orienting, and Involving Nonprofit Board Members*(Washington, DC: National Center for Nonprofit Boards, 1997), p. 32.

38. Nelson, pp. 37-38.

39. Wolf, p. 47.

40. Axelrod, p. 1.

41. Kathleen Brown Fletcher,*The Nine Keys to Successful Volunteer Programs* (Rockville, MD: The Taft Group, 1987), pp. 46-47.

42. Lucille A. Maddalena,*A Communications Manual for Nonprofit Organizations* (New York: AMACOM, 1981), p. 70.

43. Maddalena, pp. 71-72.

44. *Serving on the Board of a Tax-Exempt Organization*,p. 11.

45. Klein, p. 53.

46. Fletcher, pp. 46-47.

47. Nelson, p. 40.

48. Maddalena, p. 72.

49. O'Connell,*The Board Member's Book*,p. 65.

50. Nelson, p. 40.

51. Keegan, pp. 205-206.

52. Eadie, p. 59.

53. O'Connell,*The Board Member's Book*,p. 66.

54. Maddalena, p. 76.

55. Maddalena, p. 75.

56. Robinson, p. 21.

57. Thomas P. Holland,*How to Build a More Effective Board*(Washington, DC: National Center for Nonprofit Boards, 1996), p. 6.

58. Robinson, p. 15.

59. Maddalena, p. 76.

60. Nelson, p. 47.

61. Nelson, p. 48.

62. Keegan, p. 158.

63. O'Connell,*The Board Member's Book*,p. 67.

64. Lauer,*Communication Power*,p. 83.

65. William R. Conrad Jr. and William E. Glenn,*Effective Voluntary Board of Directors*(Athens, OH: Swallow Press, 1983), p. 158.

66. Rados, p. 443.

67. Keegan, pp. 196-200.

68. Mary Carson, "Seven Keys to Building an Effective Board,"*Discovery YMCA*, Winter 1997, p. 19.

Bibliography

Afterman, Allan B. and Rowan H. Jones.*Nonprofit Accounting and Auditing Disclosure Manual 1993.* Boston, MA: Warren Gorham Lamont, 1993.

Allen, R.R., C. David Mortensen, and Sharol Parish.*Communication: Interacting Through Speech.* Columbus, OH: Charles E. Merrill Publishing Co., 1974.

Allen, Steve. *How to Make a Speech.* New York: McGraw-Hill Book Company, 1986.

American Red Cross. *The Work of a Chapter Board: A Guide for Chapter Board Members.* Washington, DC, 1995.

America's Nonprofit Sector in Brief. Washington, DC: Independent Sector, 1998.

"Annual Reports: Not-for-Profit Organizations.*PR Tactics,* August 1997: 11-12.

The A. R. Client. Cloquet, MN: Potlach Corporation.

Arth, Marvin and Helen Ashmore.*The Newsletter Editor's Desk Book.* Third Edition. Shawnee Mission, KS: Parkway Press, 1984.

Axelrod, Nancy R. *The Chief Executive's Role in Developing the Nonprofit Board.* NCNB Governance Series New York: National Center for Nonprofit Boards, 1993.

Barry, Bryan W.*Strategic Planning Workbook for Nonprofit Organizations.*St. Paul, MN: Amherst H. Wilder, 1994.

Beach, Mark.*Newsletter Sourcebook.* Cincinnati, OH: F&W Publications, 1993.

Beebe, Steven A. and Susan J. Beebe.*Public Speaking: An Audience-Centered Approach,* Third Edition. Boston, MA: Allyn & Bacon, 1997.

Bennett, James T. "Assessing Charitable Organizations.*Consumer's Research,* May 1991: 15-19.

Bivens, Thomas. *Fundamentals of Successful Newsletters.* Lincolnwood, IL: NTC Business Books, 1993.

Bivens, Thomas. *Handbook for Public Relations Writing.* Third Edition. Lincolnwood, IL: NTC Business Books, 1995.

Blake, Barbara Radke and Barbara L. Stein.*Creating Newsletters, Brochures, and Pamphlets.* New York: Neal-Schuman Publishers, Inc., 1992.

Book, Albert C. and C. Dennis Schick.*Fundamentals of Copy & Layout.* Lincolnwood, IL: NTC Business Books, 1986.

Boyd, Stephen. "What's a Body to Do?*Public Management,* April 1996: 25-27.

*Building an Effective Employee Communications Program.*New York: PRSA, 1995.

Campbell, Karlyn Kohrs.*The Rhetorical Act.* Second Edition. New York: Wadsworth Publishing Company, 1996.

Carson, Mary. "Seven Keys to Building an Effective Board.*Discovery YMCA,* Winter 1997: 17-25.

Carver, John. *Boards That Make a Difference* San Francisco: Jossey-Bass Publishers, 1990.

Cavanaugh, Dan. *Preparing Visual Aids for Presentation* Boston: Allyn & Bacon, 1997.

Caywood, Clarke L., ed. *The Handbook of Strategic Public Relations & Integrated Communications.* New York: McGraw-Hill, 1997.

Clark, Wayne. "Nonprofits with Strong Boards Will Be Survivors. *The Business Journal,* May 19, 1997: 40.

Clark, Wayne. "Steps to Properly Ground a Nonprofit Board. *The Business Journal,* June 15, 1998: 49.

Connors, Denis. "A Fertile Annual Report Market. *Public Relations Quarterly,* Winter 1991-1992: 33-34.

Conover, Theodore E. *Graphic Communications Today,* Second Edition. New York: West Publishing Company, 1990.

Conrad, William R. and William E. Glenn. *Effective Voluntary Board of Directors* Athens, OH: Swallow Press, 1983.

Cotton, Marjorie. "Yes, I Would Like a Choice Where My Contribution Goes. *Fund Raising Management,* December 1991: 36-37.

Craig, James. *Production for the Graphic Designer* New York: Watson-Guptill Publications, 1974.

"Creating a Speakers' Bureau. *Tactics,* October 1997: 10.

Cutlip, Scott M. *Fundraising in the United States: Its Role in America's Philanthropy* New Brunswick, NJ: Transaction Publishers, 1990.

Cutlip, Scott M. and Allen H. Center. *Effective Public Relations,* Fifth Edition. Englewood Cliffs, NJ: Prentice Hall, Inc., 1982.

Devito, Joseph A. *The Elements of Public Speaking,* Fifth Edition. New York: HarperCollins College Publishers, 1994.

Douglis, Philip N. "Improving the Deadly 'Looking Down' Picture. *IABC Communication World,* March 1990: 40.

Douglis, Philip N. "Get Up, Get Down for Better Portraits. *IABC Communication World,* January 1991: 40.

Douglis, Philip N. "Improving the Talking-Head Shot. *IABC Communication World,* June-July 1991: 52.

Douglis, Philip N. "Natural Response Key to Informal Portraits. *IABC Communication World,* November 1991: 42.

Douglis, Philip N. "When Sequence and Placement Make the Point. *IABC Communication World,* August 1992: 31.

Douglis, Philip N. "Beat the Gather-Round-the-Desk Cliché. *IABC Communication World,* June-July 1993: 58.

Douglis, Philip N. "Cover Meetings with Varied Viewpoints. *IABC Communication World,* September 1993: 49.

Douglis, Philip N. "Good Photographers Climb High, Shoot Down. *IABC Communication World,* December 1993: 42.

Douglis, Philip N. "Improving the Boring Machine Shot. *IABC Communication World,* April 1996: 43.

Douglis, Philip N. "Where You Stand Determines What You Say.*IABC Communication World,* June-July 1996: 73.

Douglis, Philip N. "Intimacy: The Up-Close and Personal Picture.*IABC Communication World,* December-January 1996-1997: 41.

Douglis, Philip N. "How Eyes Can Express Meaning in Pictures.*IABC Communication World,* April-May 1997: 41.

Drucker, Peter F. "What Can Nonprofits Teach Us?*Review,* May 1990: 23-44.

Dwyer, Karen Kangas.*Conquer Your Speechfright.* New York: Harcourt Brace College Publishers, 1998.

Eadie, Douglas C.*Boards That Work: A Practical Guide to Building Effective Association Boards.* Washington, DC: American Society of Association Executives, 1994.

Epstein, Marc J. "The Fall of Corporate Charitable Contributions.*Public Relations Quarterly,* Summer 1993: 37-39.

Fanson, Barbara.*Producing a First-Class Newsletter.* Bellingham, WA: Self-Counsel Press, 1994.

"Financial World Annual Report Competition Winners.*Financial World,* November 18, 1996: 96-101.

Fitting the Pieces Together: Publicity Manual. Knoxville, TN: Public Relations Society of America, Knoxville Chapter, 1981.

Fletcher, Kathleen Brown.*The Nine Keys to Successful Volunteer Programs.* Rockville, MD: The Taft Group, 1987.

Floyd, Elaine.*Marketing with Newsletters,* Second Edition. St. Louis, MO: Newsletter Resources, 1997.

Forward, David C.*Heroes After Hours: Extraordinary Acts of Employee Volunteerism.* San Francisco, CA: Jossey-Bass Inc., 1994.

Foster, John S. "Lessons Learned from the United Way Scandal.*Convene,* June 1995: 37-40.

Fulkerson, Jennifer. "How Investors Use Annual Reports.*American Demographics,* May 1996: 16-19.

Getting Into Print. Ann Arbor, MI: Promotion Perspectives, 1990.

Getty, Cheryl. "Planning Successfully for Succession Planning.*Training and Development,* November 1993: 31-33.

Giving and Volunteering in the United States: Findings from a National Survey, 1996 Edition. Washington, DC: Independent Sector, 1996.

Gladis, Stephen D. *The Ten Commandments for Public Speakers.* Amherst, MA: Human Resource Development Press, Inc., 1990.

"Good Captions—Good in Content and in Form—Are Potent Typographic Tools for Readership."*Editor's Workshop,* February 1992: 8-9.

Graphics Master 2. Los Angeles, CA: Dean Lem Associates, 1977.

Gronbeck, Bruce E., Kathleen German, Douglas Ehninger, and Alan Monroe.*Principles of Speech Communication,* Twelfth Edition. New York: HarperCollins College Publishers, 1995.

Grossmann, Joe and David Doty.*Newsletters from the Desktop,* Second Edition. Chapel Hill, NC: Ventana Press, Inc., 1994.

*Guidelines for Publishing a Minimum Annual Report*Washington, DC: Council on Foundations, 1982.

Haggerty, Alfred G. "Annual Reports Can Cost Big Bucks."*National Underwriter,* February 16, 1987: 57-62.

Harte, Thomas B., Carolyn Keefe, and Bob R. Derryberry.*The Complete Book of Speechwriting for Students and Professionals,*Third Edition. Edina, MN: Burgess International Group, Inc., 1992.

Hasek, Glenn. "Adding Art to Numbers."*Industry Week,* November 17, 1997: 122-125.

Hayes, Cassandra. "Making Connections: Passing on the Baton."*Black Enterprise,* September 1996: 52.

Hamilton, Edward A.*Newsletter Design.* New York: Van Nostrand Reinhold, 1996.

Hill, Bill, and Charlynn Ross.*Public Speaking: Process and Product.*Dubuque, IA: Kendall Hunt Publishing Company, 1993.

Hodgkinson, Virginia A.*Nonprofit Almanac, 1996-1997.*San Francisco: Jossey-Bass, Incorporated, 1996.

Hoff, Ron.*I Can See You Naked.* New York: Andrews and McMeel, 1988.

Holland, Thomas P.*How to Build a More Effective Board.*Washington, DC: National Center for Nonprofit Boards, 1996.

Horvath, Terri.*Spread the Word: How to Promote Nonprofit Groups with a Network of Speakers.* Indianapolis, IN: Publishing Resources, 1995.

Howard, Carole M. and Wilma K. Mathews.*On Deadline: Managing Media Relations,* Second Edition. Prospect Heights, IL: Waveland Press, Inc., 1994.

*How to Conduct a Readership Survey.*New York: Editor's Newsletter, n.d.

*How to Plan Printing.*Boston, MA: S.D. Warren Company, 1988.

Hudson, Howard Penn.*Publishing Newsletters,*Revised Edition. New York: Charles Scribner's Sons, 1988.

Hunt, Todd and Grunig, James E.*Public Relations Techniques.* New York: Harcourt Brace Publishers, 1994.

*Investor Relations Surveys: Annual Reports.*Vienna, VA: National Investor Relations Institute, 1996.

Johanek, John. "Five Design Myths That Can Ruin Your Newsletter."*PR Tactics,* August 1995: 10.

Kaplan, Ann E., ed.*Giving USA 1996. The Annual Report on Philanthropy for the Year 1995.* New York: AAFRC Trust for Philanthropy, 1996.

Kaplan, Ann E., ed.*Giving USA 1997.* New York: American Association of Fundraising Counsel, 1997.

Kaplan, Ann E.*Giving USA 1998.*New York: AARFC Trust for Philanthropy, 1998.

Kaplan, Ann E.*Giving USA 1999.*New York: AARFC Trust for Philanthropy, 1999.

Keegan, P. Burke.*Fundraising for Non-Profits.* New York: HarperPerennial, 1990.

Kelley, Joseph J.*Speechwriting: A Handbook for All Occasions.*New York: Times Minnon, 1980.

Kendall, Jane. "The Makings of a Good Nonprofit Board Member."*The Business Journal,* February 9, 1998: 45.

Kendall, Robert. *Public Relations Campaign Strategies: Planning for Implementation,* Second Edition. New York: HarperCollins College Publishers, 1996.

"Kicking the Photographic Cliché."*Editor's Workshop,*February 1992: 8-9.

Kile, Robert W. and J. Michael Loscavio.*Strategic Board Recruitment: The Not-for-Profit Model.* Gaithersburg, MD: Aspen Publishers, 1996.

Klein, Kim. *Fundraising for Social Change,*Third Edition. Inverness, CA: Chardon Press, 1994.

Kotler, Philip and Alan Andreasen.*Strategic Marketing for Nonprofit Organizations,* Fourth Edition. Englewood Cliffs, NJ: Prentice Hall, Inc., 1991.

Kotler, Philip and Alan Andreasen.*Strategic Marketing for Nonprofit Organizations,* Fifth Edition. Upper Saddle River, NJ: Prentice Hall, 1996.

Lauer, Larry D. *Communication Power: Energizing Your Nonprofit Organization* Gaithersburg, MD: Aspen Publishers, 1997.

Lauer, Larry D. "How Well Does Your Board Communicate?"*Nonprofit World,* March-April 1997: 16-17.

Lucas, Stephen E.*The Art of Public Speaking,*Sixth Edition. Boston, MA: McGraw-Hill, 1998.

Maddalena, Lucille A.*A Communications Manual for Nonprofit Organizations*New York: AMACOM, 1981.

Mancuso, Anthony.*How to Form a Nonprofit Corporation,*Second Edition. Berkeley, CA: Nolo Press, 1994.

Mandel, Steve.*Effective Presentation Skills,*Revised Edition. Menlo Park, CA: Crisp Titles, 1993.

Marino, Sal. "Straight Talk."*Industry Week,* May 5, 1997: 12.

Marken, G.A. "Public Relations Photos . . . Beyond the Written Word."*Public Relations Quarterly,*Summer 1993: 7-12.

Maxymuk, John. *Using Desktop Publishing to Create Newsletters, Handouts, and Web Pages* New York: Neal-Schuman Publishers, Inc., 1997.

May, Debra Hart.*Proofreading: Plain and Simple* Franklin Lakes, NJ: Career Press, 1997.

McCarthy, Edward H.*Speechwriting: A Professional Step-by-Step Guide for Executives.* Dayton, OH: The Executive Speaker Company, 1989.

Montana, Patrick. *Marketing in Nonprofit Organizations* New York: AMACOM, 1978.

Moore, Pamela. "CD Won't Go Platinum, But Heck, It's an Annual Report."*The Charlotte Observer,*March 18, 1996: 3D.

Morreale, Sherwyn P. and Courtland L. Bovee.*Excellence in Public Speaking* New York: Harcourt Brace College Publishers, 1998.

Murray, Milton and Ken Turpen. "Annual Reports that Raise Money."*Fund Raising Management,* June 1996: 48.

Nauffts, Mitchell F., ed.*Foundation Fundamentals: A Guide for Grantseekers,*Fifth Edition. New York: The Foundation Center, 1994.

Nelson, Judith Grummon.*Six Keys to Recruiting, Orienting, and Involving Nonprofit Board Members* Washington, DC: National Center for Nonprofit Boards, 1997.

Nelson, Peggy *How to Create Powerful Newsletters.*Chicago: Bonus Books, Inc., 1993.

Nelson, Roy Paul.*Publication Design,*Second Edition. Dubuque, IA: Wm. C. Brown Company Publishers, 1978.

Nelson, Roy Paul. "The Caption Challenge."*IABC Communication World,*December 1993: 44.

Newman, Joyce. "Speaker Training: Twenty-Five Experts on Substance and Style." *Public Relations Quarterly,*Summer 1988: 15-20.

*The 1997 Potlatch Annual Report Show: The Essentials*Cloquet, MN: Potlatch, 1997.

"No Thanks."*Industry Week,* April 12, 1997: 12.

Nucifora, Alf. "Your Newsletter Can Be a Valuable Tool If Done Right.*Business Journal,* March 31, 1997: 23.

Nucifora, Alf. "Nonprofits Learn Ropes of Marketing."*Business Journal,* April 13, 1998: 21-23.

O'Connell, Brian.*Effective Leadership in Voluntary Organizations*New York: Walker and Company, 1981.

O'Connell, Brian. *The Board Member's Book,* Second Edition. New York: The Foundation Center, 1993.

Olenick, Arnold J. and Philip R. Olenick*A Nonprofit Organization Operating Manual: Planning for Survival and Growth*New York: The Foundation Center, 1991.

Parker, Roger C.*Newsletters from the Desktop* Chapel Hill, NC: Ventana Press, 1990.

Promoting Issues and Ideas: A Guide to Public Relations for Nonprofit Organizations. New York: The Foundation Center, 1987.

Rados, David L.*Marketing for Nonprofit Organizations,*Second Edition. Westport, CT: Auburn House, 1996.

Raymond, Larry.*Reinventing Communication: A Guide to Using Visual Language for Planning, Problem Solving, and Reengineering*Milwaukee, WI: ASQC Quality Press, 1994.

*Riley v. National Federation of the Blind of North Carolina, Inc.*87-328 487 U.S. 781, 108 SCT 2867, L101, Ed. 2d, p. 669(March 23, 1988) (June 29, 1988).

Robinson, Andy.*Grassroots Grants: An Activist's Guide to Proposal Writing*Berkeley, CA: Chardon Press, 1996.

Robinson, Maureen K.*Developing the Nonprofit Board*Washington, DC: National Center for Nonprofit Boards, 1994.

Rosso, Henry A.*Achieving Excellence in Fundraising: A Comprehensive Guide to Principles, Strategies, and Methods* San Francisco: Jossey-Bass Publishers, 1991.

Rosso, Henry A.*Rosso on Fundraising* San Francisco, CA: Jossey-Bass Publishers, 1996.

Salamon, Lester M. and Helmut K. Anheier.*The Emerging Nonprofit Sector: An Overview.* New York: Manchester University Press, 1996.

Samuelson, J. "Close to the Lunatic Edge."*Newsweek,* April 21, 1997: 53.

*Securities and Exchange Act of 1934*Section 14. Securities and Exchange Commission, U.S. Federal Government, Washington, DC.

Seitel, Fraser P. *The Practice of Public Relations,* Seventh Edition. Upper Saddle River, NJ: Prentice Hall, 1998.

Seltzer, Michael. *Securing Your Organization's Future: A Complete Guide to Fundraising Strategies* New York: The Foundation Center, 1987.

Serving on the Board of a Tax-Exempt Organization: A Guide for New Directors Chicago: Grant Thornton, 1993.

"Short, Sweet and Oh So Cheap." *Forbes,* June 2, 1997: 161.

Skloot, Edward, ed. *Nonprofit Entrepreneur: Creating Ventures to Earn Income* New York: The Foundation Center, 1988.

Skolnik, Rayna. "Rebuilding Trust: Nonprofits Act to Boost Reputations." *Public Relations Journal,* September 1993: 29-32.

Sparks, Suzanne and Melody Templeton. "Combating Your Fear of Presentations." *Tactics,* January 1998, p. 5, 18.

"Speakers Get More Mileage from Your Speech." *Industry Week,* November 17, 1997: 8.

Squires, Conrad. *Teach Yourself to Write Irresistible Fundraising Letters* Chicago: Precept Press, Inc., 1993.

Statistical Abstract of United States: 1997 Washington, DC: Bureau of Census, U.S. Department of Commerce, 1997.

Steele, Elizabeth. "Ten Ways to Get More from an Annual Report." *Public Relations Quarterly,* Fall 1990: 25-26.

Stern, Gary. *Marketing Workbook for Nonprofit Organizations* St. Paul, MN: Amherst H. Wilder Foundation, 1994.

Stern, Gary. *Marketing Workbook for Nonprofit Organizations, Vol. II: Mobilize People for Marketing Success.* St. Paul, MN: Amherst H. Wilder Foundation Publishing Center, 1997.

A Study of Corporate Annual Reports Cloquet, MN: Potlatch Corporation, 1995.

"Survey: Annual Reports Repurposed from Print to Web Are on Rise." *Graphic Design,* June 1997: 22.

"Survey: Annuals Up on the Web." *Graphic Design,* November 1996: 26.

Thompson, William. *Targeting the Message: A Receiver-Centered Process for Public Relations Writing.* White Plains, NY: Longman Publishers, 1996.

Umiker, William O. "Succession Planning: A Manager's Guide." *Medical Laboratory Observer,* September 1994: 40-42.

Wargula, Carol A. "Funding Opportunities Newsletters: How Useful Are They." *SRA Journal,* Summer 1991: 35.

Wheildon, Colin. *Type & Layout* Berkeley, CA: Strathmoor Press, 1995.

Wilcox, Dennis L., Phillip H. Ault, and Warren K. Agee. *Public Relations: Strategies and Tactics,* Fourth Edition. New York: HarperCollins College Publishers, 1995.

Wilcox, Dennis L., Phillip H. Ault, and Warren K. Agee. *Public Relations: Strategies and Tactics,* Fifth Edition. New York: Addison Wesley Longman, Inc., 1998.

Wilcox, Dennis and Lawrence W. Nolte. *Fundamentals of Public Relations: Professional Guidelines, Concepts and Integrations* Second Edition. New York: Pergamon Press, 1979.

Wilcox, Dennis and Lawrence W. Nolte.*Public Relations: Writing and Media Techniques,* Second Edition. New York: HarperCollins College Publishers, 1995.

Williams, Patricia A.*Creating and Producing the Perfect Newsletter.*Glenview, IL: Scott, Foresman, and Company, 1990.

Wilson, Laurie J.*Strategic Program Planning,*Second Edition. Dubuque, IA: Kendall-Hunt Publishing Company, 1997.

Wolf, Thomas.*Managing a Nonprofit Organization.*New York: Fireside, 1990.

Wright, Nanette.*Blueline Guideline* New York: Wright Communications, 1998.

Zelazny, Gene.*Say It with Charts,* Third Edition. Chicago: Irwin Professional Publishing, 1996.

Index

Page numbers followed by the letter "f" indicate forms; those followed by the letter "i" indicate illustrations; and those followed by the letter "t" indicate tables.

An environmentally friendly book printed and bound in England by www.printondemand-worldwide.com

This book is made entirely of chain-of-custody materials

#0219 - 020512 - C0 - 212/152/13 - PB